Beyond Sight

The Hidden History of Remote Viewing

and Psycho Energetics

Tony Rodrigues

Forward by Jackie Kenner

Tony Rodrigues isn't just a friend; he's more like family - a soul sibling with whom I share a bond that defies explanation. Our connection began with a simple plea for help, a message I sent out into the digital void in search of understanding my disorienting recall experience.

Back then, the world of secret programs and covert black budget projects was completely foreign to me. But Tony's wealth of knowledge and his personal experiences in these shadowy realms became a guiding light, leading me down a path of healing and discovery.

As our friendship grew, we started to share our research on topics like astral travel, psychic training, and the mysterious workings of the mind. While my experiences at the time were limited to my adulthood psychic breakthrough, Tony's story painted a picture of a childhood marred by abduction and exploitation in military projects.

If you're new to Tony's story, start with his first book, *Ceres Colony Cavalier*, and follow it up with the sequel, *Project Starmaker*. These two volumes provide the essential backstory to Tony's extraordinary experiences. I encourage you to read them with an open mind and an active third eye. While much of the relevant evidence of Tony's story is forthcoming, the complete backstory of Tony's involvement will enhance your appreciation of this book.

I'll never forget the shock of learning about the scientist behind the cruel experiments Tony endured at Inyokern Airport. A scientist still actively contributing to Remote Viewing research to this day. Despite my reservations, Tony's determination to share his truth has been unwavering—a bold statement against those who sought to silence him.

Beyond the tales of Tony's suffering lies a message of empowerment. Remote Viewing, once shrouded in secrecy, emerges as a tool for self-discovery and growth - a practice Tony has been teaching for years, now laid out for you in these pages.

So, I invite you to join us on this journey - to explore the depths of your own consciousness, to embrace the power within you, and to step boldly into a world of endless possibility. For within these pages lies not only a story but a challenge - a challenge to awaken, to transcend, and to become the architects of our own destinies.

Table of Contents

I would like to dedicate this book to the lessons in life that both my closest loved ones and my worst enemies have taught me. Without whom I would have never grown to be what I am today.

The people that have done harm to me showed me a world that requires my constant attention and focus.

My loved ones have healed me from that harm done, and showed me a world worth living in.

To my daughters I hope that I can reflect the inspiration they have given me. That they can live their lives vigilant and loving, and they understand what they have meant to me.

Disclaimer - I used chat gpt to dig up the historical information in the *first* chapter of this book and wash it for punctuation. Also I went through all the A.I. generated content and rewrote it to sound less like a pretentious d-bag. There is a direct A.I. quote in the countermeasures chapter to illustrate how easy that information is to obtain. To be clear - I wrote this book. To me A.I. writing is just like a salesman trying to stroke your ego and use big words to sound competent.

It was a handy tool to correct punctuation and dig up some information for the First and Countermeasures chapters. I think it is important that authors disclose any and all influences on their works by A.I. This is the world we now live in.

Chapter 1: History of Psy

In all of human history, there exists a phenomenon that is as intriguing as it is contentious - remote viewing. Evoking images of mystics peering into crystal balls, it is, in reality, much different from such arcane associations. Remote viewing is a practice or ability to perceive or describe details about a distant or unseen target, including locations, objects, or people, without the use of the known senses or physical interaction. It challenges the current understanding of conventional boundaries of time and space, suggesting that the human mind can access information about remote geographical locations or events separated by vast distances or even time itself. The very notion of remote viewing is challenging to many aspects of mainstream science. Nevertheless, access to target data is relatively easy to replicate and must be taken seriously.

The genesis of remote viewing as a concept and practice can be traced back to ancient civilizations, where seers and prophets claimed to possess the ability to see beyond the visible, into realms and realities beyond the reach of ordinary perception. However, the modern iteration of remote viewing, particularly its scientific exploration and application, began in the mid-20th century, during a period marked by the Cold War and a burgeoning interest in espionage and intelligence gathering.

The term "remote viewing" was coined in the early 1970s at the Stanford Research Institute (SRI) in California, where researchers Russell Targ and Harold Puthoff embarked on experiments to investigate the potential of human consciousness to perceive distant locations, or "targets," beyond the range of traditional sensory capabilities. Their pioneering work sought to place remote viewing within a framework of scientific inquiry, rigorously testing individuals who claimed to possess such abilities under controlled conditions. The results, often met with skepticism and controversy, nevertheless laid the groundwork for a field of study that challenges our understanding of the limits of human perception and cognition.

Although it was coined as a term and seriously looked into in the 1970s and 80s, the first known mention of it I came across was in one of the many declassified documents I have looked through over the years while gathering information supporting my own involvement in an experimental program in the 1980s.

*Be advised: All of the documents from the freedom of information act that I have collected for this book can be searched for by the number address on the page i.e. :
CIA-RDP96-00789R001001420001-3 entered in the search at:
https://www.cia.gov/readingroom/home
would find this one for instance*:

The first recorded experiment of psi involved a military intelligence application of remote-viewing. Back in 550 B.C. King Croesus of Lydia felt threatened by the increasing power of the Persians. He needed to know what they were planning. Historians give us a detailed account of just what happened. Croesus sought an oracle who could somehow perceive his enemies plans; an oracle with proven psychic abilities. So he devised a simple test. He dispatched messengers throughout the ancient world to visit

5

different oracles and ask for a written description of Croesus' activities at a specified time and day. The oracle at Delphi responded:

> I can count the sands, and I can measure the ocean; I have ears for the silent, and know what the dumb man nameth; Lo! On my sense there striketh the smell of a shell-covered tortoise, Boiling now on a fire, with the flesh of a lamb, in a caldron-- Brass is the vessel below, and brass is the cover above it (41:12).

Only the Delphi oracle provided the correct response, for on the specified day, Croesus did something he thought

> most impossible for anyone to conceive of his doing...He took a tortoise and a lamb, and cutting them in pieces with his own hands, boiled them both together in a brazen caldron, covered over with a lid that was also brass (41:12).

Croesus' 550 B.C. experiment convinced him remote-viewing worked (for the Delphi oracle), and provided him a significant intelligence force multiplier against his Persian enemies. How far have we advanced since then?

14

At its core, remote viewing is predicated on the belief that the human mind is capable of transcending its physical confines, tapping into a universal source of information - a collective unconscious or a quantum field of interconnectedness - that binds all of existence. Proponents argue that, with training and practice, anyone can develop the skill to access this reservoir of knowledge, effectively erasing the barriers that define the known and the unknown.

The methodologies of remote viewing have evolved over the years, from the initial protocols established by Targ and Puthoff to more refined techniques designed to enhance accuracy and repeatability. These methodologies typically involve a viewer, a target, and a series of steps or stages through which the viewer attempts to describe the target, which is unknown to them and often located at a significant distance. The process is meticulously documented, and the results are compared against the actual characteristics or events related to the target, providing a measure of the viewer's accuracy.

Despite its potential implications for intelligence gathering, scientific research, and our understanding of consciousness, remote viewing remains a polarizing subject. Critics dismiss it as pseudoscience, citing a lack of replicable evidence and the influence of sensory cues or information leakage on the results of experiments. My personal experience, as I currently host a remote viewing group, is quite the opposite. It IS very replicable and something that everyone can do. Advocates continue to explore its applications, from archaeological discoveries to solving crimes, arguing that remote viewing represents an untapped capacity of the human mind. I personally state as often as I can that we have many voices that chime into our thought process—a fearful one, telling us this is going to fail, and a careless one, saying just do it anyway. However, we have the correct inner voice of intuition that often sounds crazy but is correct 100% of the time. Remote viewing lets you identify that voice time and time again. So getting to know your own personal intuition is far more valuable than spying on the Soviets.

As we stand on the threshold of this uncharted territory, the history of remote viewing invites us to reconsider the boundaries of human potential and the mysteries that lie just beyond the veil of our everyday perception. It challenges us to question the limits of what we know and to imagine what might be possible if we could truly see without looking. In fact, as this book will demonstrate, remote viewing is just the tip of the iceberg. There are much more unbelievable abilities that can be learned building off of the same methods.

The term "remote viewing" didn't encompass all of the things that the Stanford Research Institute and the U.S. military had discovered were possible in the early 1970s. After developing it they renamed it to "Psycho Energetics" in the early 1980's

For most of my life, I believed completely normal things—things that were only taught in school or on TV - the same way we all do. My mother was a devout Christian woman, but she still believed in psychic phenomena, having experienced much of it herself. She instilled that in us kids - that these things were not reported by the mainstream, not acknowledged by academia, but existed and were profound nonetheless.

I would always sit on the sidelines, believing that I had nothing pertaining to this phenomenon. Always thinking that abilities were for the "pros" and I was in the crowd. Psychic phenomena didn't pertain to me because I was normal. However, as I chronicled in my first book, *Ceres Colony Cavalier*, at a point in my life I regained memories of being abducted and participating in black programs developing exactly that - "Psycho Energetic" abilities. I found that there is much more possible once you develop the ability to simply view a target.

I'm not going to kid you and pretend that the things I say in my book that I remember are easy to believe. I remember a society that lives among our elites that not only partakes in psychic ability but is built around it, as well as a society that has access to space and deep space trade with extraterrestrial species on a near-infinite scale. Yeah, hard to say out loud, let alone rationalize.

In an attempt to find evidence to present the things I remember to the public and not sound absolutely delusional, I am constantly researching what I remember.

A trip to one of the places I remember vividly was my first stop in the twenty-year tour. I not only had accurate memories of the area and the remains of buildings on the site, but I also found breadcrumbs of a paper trail into the project I was in. The dates of my memories line up, as well as many key details.

The realization of the technologies and brutality of the research were shocking to recall. However, the implications, I believe, have huge ramifications on literally everyone on the planet and the human experience as a whole. Always being an optimist, I feel this knowledge is worth sharing. I decided to look into the history of remote viewing, which is just a category of psy abilities, or psycho-energetics.

Just how long has this been going on? The company that had personnel in my program had been researching remote viewing funded by the DOD in the early 1970s. However, human psy abilities seem to have gone all the way back into history for as far as we have recorded it. Let's look at a brief history of this phenomenon, as well as a look into where we are today with psycho-energetics and what I remember of my time working for the Ceres Colony Corporation. That may give us a "view" into the future of the human experience.

Chapter 2: His Story

If we really want to begin at the start of it all, the phenomenon of Psycho Energetics goes back all the way into written history. Throughout human history, we have records of people demonstrating fantastic abilities both mentally and intuitively: oracles, psychics, healers, precognition, and even stories of people who could move objects or teleport, disappearing and reappearing immediately far away. These are not new phenomena; they have been with us the entire time. As long as people have gazed at the sky, we have had psychic phenomena.

In the Paleolithic era, we have cave scenes that depict supernatural beliefs.

Shamans and spiritual leaders have always been considered conduits between the physical and the spiritual realms, often employing altered states of consciousness to receive visions and insights. They used natural methods such as herbs, psychedelics, and even areas of low oxygen to induce states of mind that allowed them to access realms outside of our reality.

In ancient Mesopotamia, priests and priestesses were intermediaries between the gods and humans; they used many forms of divination, such as reading the entrails of animals and interpreting patterns of the stars, to gain insights into the future.

The ancient Egyptians held strong beliefs in the afterlife and the metaphysical. The concept of "ka," a form of life force or spiritual double, is well documented in their religious texts. Priests used rituals and spells to communicate with the gods and the deceased, often seeking guidance through dreams and visions. This is starting to sound familiar, but in reality, we are talking about 6,000 years ago at this point. I have my own theory about Egyptian monuments being used to amplify psychoenergetic abilities. These days, who doesn't have a theory about the pyramids like that? We will circle back to that.

In ancient Greece, the Oracle of Delphi is perhaps one of the most famous examples of psychic phenomena. Pythia, the high priestess of the Temple of Apollo, would enter into a trance-like state and deliver prophecies believed to be messages from the gods. When we talk about remote viewing, some of it works the same way - it all begins with meditation or entering a trance-like state. There have been studies concluding that the oracle at Delphi was put in a low-oxygen environment under the temple, achieving a trance-like state. The prophetic accuracy of the young women in this temple is legendary.

In ancient India and China, the concept of life force - prana in Hinduism and chi in Taoism - was central to their spiritual philosophies. Practices like yoga and meditation were designed to harness this energy and attain higher states of consciousness, often leading to experiences described as mystical or precognitive.

Religious texts and mythologies throughout history are full of accounts of miracles, visions, and prophecies. From the biblical prophets to Norse seers, these stories have shaped our understanding of the physical realm, often blurring the lines between divine intervention and human ability. If you really ask around when you get close to somebody and become friends, everybody has a tale of an experience that was supernatural. Maybe they turned left instead of right, avoiding calamity, or knew to call a friend who was in distress. A voice in their head guided them to make a decision that made all the difference in the world. Everyone's got one of these stories; it's a common thing - it's how we work. Science has been held from us.

Understanding this historical context is crucial for an exploration of remote viewing or psychoenergetics. When we consider what the government has done to research this and, in fact, perfected many aspects of it, we know from declassified documents that this is just as natural as breathing, sleeping, or eating. Psy phenomena, whatever you choose to call it, is part of the human experience and always has been.

Let's go further. It's important to see through all of history and look at all the times because at some point, it was roped, subdued, and hidden from the public. In fact, there's a large campaign to hide this phenomenon from the everyday person even today.

The Middle Ages and the Renaissance were periods of stark contrasts when it came to psychic phenomena and practices like remote viewing. On one hand, these eras were marked by the persecution of individuals who believed they possessed psychic abilities; on the other, they saw the rise of scholarly interest in the occult and the metaphysical.

With the fall of the Roman Empire and the rise of Christianity, the perception of psychic phenomena underwent a significant transformation. The church often labeled psychic abilities as heretical, associating them with witchcraft and demonic possession. The infamous witch trials across Europe serve as grim reminders of this period.

Despite orthodoxy prevailing in this effort of suppression, the Middle Ages also saw a rapid growth of alchemy and astrology, which were considered legitimate sciences at the time and were often practiced by scholars and clergy alike. Alchemists like Paracelsus wrote extensively on the astral body, a concept closely related to modern understandings of psychic phenomena.

As I've been researching the information for this part of the book, I've been shocked at the things I found. Systemic practices linked to the occult bleed through when you start to look at battles that have been fought. Take, for instance, the fall of Carthage, where ritual human sacrifice had been banned for upwards of 80 years by the time of its fall but was prevalent globally at the time.

When the Romans had surrounded the city and defeat was inevitable, the Carthaginians began to sacrifice their young in a blood ritual, possibly to try to find some way out. There are documented accounts of it. Why would that become a logical option? They only sacrificed the youngest. If they were trying to avoid slavery, they would have had a much larger massacre, but only the young children were sacrificed.

Could there have been a Psycho Energetic result they were hoping for?
There are great studies about the incredible results and accuracy of children in NDE experiences. Was this a desperate attempt to solve an unsolvable life or death situation?

When you look at the phenomenon of ritual human sacrifice globally, there's a story there that we're unaware of. It was as if they were sacrificing their children for some kind of favor from the other side, some kind of insight on how to survive for themselves - as if there's a science to it.

In fact, when you look at Christianity, one of the major by-products of the Catholic Church's sprawl across the world was the replacement of ritual human sacrifice with communion. "You'll drink of my blood and eat of my body" with bread and wine. That's what that was about. They asked Jesus if they should eat him at the Last Supper. That was really what that conversation was, and he said no, from now on, you'll have wine as blood and bread as his body. Catholicism did exactly that everywhere it went - it told them they were to stop the actual practice of ritual human sacrifice.

The Vatican was also able to acquire most of the knowledge and even monuments like Obelisks from Luxor and the ancient world while they stamped out sacrifices. How much

Psy knowledge could they have amassed? I was once asked in a public forum by someone who was a descendant of an American Indian tribe to show evidence of ritual human sacrifice among the American Indians. In fact, it was very easy to find evidence that the Mississippian Indians practiced ritual human sacrifice. A lot of people are unaware that the Irish did as well, along with the pagans across Europe. Certainly, in the Middle East and around the Mediterranean, many cultures practiced ritual human sacrifice - the Hawaiians, the Philippines, Malaysia, Papua New Guinea (still does in parts), Easter Island had accounts of it, as well as South America. It was a global practice and it doesn't make any sense to us in today's society. It's as if there was a technology of consciousness that accompanies it.

I have personally witnessed many forms of death: plants, insects, animals, and humans. I can say without a doubt that there is a glitch in reality when a human passes. The volume of the consciousness that changes states of existence at that moment seems to alter aspects of reality for a brief time. There are in fact, forms of Psycho Energetics that have been documented around near-death experiences that seem to be tied to U.S. government research. I will cover that later in this book.

But for now, back to the timeline of human psy behavior throughout history. What seems to be taking shape is not only the fact that entire societies in the distant past had a grasp of human psychic, psycho-energetic abilities, but they had a profound understanding and a science of them.

The revival of classical knowledge and the advent of humanism during the Renaissance marked a turning point. Scholars began to study psychic phenomena more openly. Figures like Marsilio Ficino and Giovanni Pico della Mirandola wrote about the Hermetic traditions, which included practices that could be considered precursors to remote viewing. During this period, secret societies like the Rosicrucians and the Freemasons played a crucial role in preserving and transmitting esoteric knowledge. There's a lot of stigma and negative bias around these fraternities or societies. Whether or not that's true, one thing is for sure: they had found a way to become appealing to the everyday man. People who were Christian, Protestant, Jewish, Arabic, Muslim - all alike - are members of these societies. It seems they've passed on ancient traditions steeped in mysticism that the members may not be aware of. These organizations often delved into metaphysical studies, including the exploration of psychic abilities.

The Renaissance also laid the groundwork for the Scientific Revolution. Empirical methods gained prominence, and psychic phenomena began to be scrutinized more critically. This led to some debunking but also paved the way for regular scientific investigations in the future. The Middle Ages and the Renaissance were periods of both darkness and enlightenment for the study of psychic phenomena and psychoenergetics. The era was characterized by tension between religious orthodoxy and scholarly curiosity, a tension that would continue to shape discourse around psychic abilities and remote viewing for centuries.

The 18th and 19th centuries were pivotal in shaping our modern understanding of psychic phenomena. This is an area of great curiosity to myself. Testimonies of secret space programs that began in the early 1920s are rumored to have stemmed from psychic contact or channeling with extraterrestrials to attain high technology. It allowed certain secret societies to actually attain interstellar flight. This is a very debated, very heated, and very researched topic and time frame. When we look at it, even aside from our own direction of research or, dare I say, even conspiracy, it's ridiculous how broad that term is.

The era witnessed the birth of psychology as a scientific discipline and the emergence of parapsychology, which sought to study phenomena like remote viewing through empirical methods. Little did I know that I would be swept into one of these programs in the early 80s, unknowingly participating in the advancement of psychoenergetics.

The Age of Enlightenment brought about a focus on reason and scientific inquiry. Philosophers like Immanuel Kant began to explore the nature of human consciousness and its limits, indirectly influencing the study of psychic phenomena. Kant's work on metaphysics questioned the boundaries of human perception, laying philosophical groundwork for future research. Franz Mesmer's theory of animal magnetism gained considerable attention in the 18th century. Although later discredited, Mesmer's work was one of the first attempts to study psychic phenomena like clairvoyance under controlled conditions. His practices evolved into what we now know as hypnotism, a tool still used in parapsychological research. When you think about hypnotic regression and how many people are being trained and practicing it, you have to think back to the work of animal magnetism by Franz Mesmer.

Founded in 1882, the Society for Psychical Research (SPR) in London marked a significant step towards the scientific study of psychic phenomena. Researchers like Frederick W. H. Myers and William James conducted experiments to test the validity of telepathy, precognition, and other psychic abilities.

Researching this for myself, for my own book and my own account of what I experienced, I look back on all this information and think, they didn't show us this in school. There's been debunking all along but also continuous interest. Much like ufology, people who subscribe to, study, and watch the material tend to be people who have had something happen in their own lives. People who have witnessed something that was not supposed to happen tend to be the ones in the audience, probably the ones reading this book. For the most part, people who have never had anything out of the ordinary happen to them don't subscribe to curiosities outside of their own experiences, and that's exactly what's going on with remote viewing and parapsychology.

When we look at the subject of psychoanalysis, it has brought another dimension to the study of psychic phenomena. Sigmund Freud and Carl Jung were influential in this. While Freud was quite skeptical - and frankly, the more I look into his career, the less I'm a fan - Carl Jung was more open to the idea. Jung's concept of the collective unconscious and his work on synchronicity offered a psychological framework for understanding psychic experiences. In fact, my own work and research have led me to believe that there is a collective unconsciousness that remains entirely neutral and that we access quite often, almost every day while we sleep, seemingly to get permission for actions that are about to happen. There is an unconsciousness outside of timespace, or the array, or the absolute infinity, or whatever you would choose to call the place just outside of timespace. It has many names, but it's important to realize that we can access it in our theta state, just before we wake up, and where we communicate with others in a completely unfiltered, neutral, and unbiased manner. We achieve forms of permission. It's how people meet each other and seemingly know each other already. It's where the co-creative aspects of our lives happen.

As we get into the 20th century and the research around psychic phenomena, there were some major setbacks. The early 20th century was dominated by behaviorism, a psychological approach that focuses solely on observable behavior, dismissing internal experiences like thoughts or psychic phenomena. This had a horrific chilling effect on the study of psychic abilities, relegating it to the fringes of scientific inquiry, and for the most part, that's where we find it today, even though the evidence is shocking. As I'll cover shortly in this book, the government has perfected a great amount of psychoenergetic phenomena.

J. B. Rhine, a psychologist at Duke University, challenged the behaviorist paradigm by conducting controlled experiments on extrasensory perception and psychokinesis. His work laid the foundation for modern parapsychology and opened the door for scientific investigations into psychic phenomena. He was the one who developed the Zener cards—five distinct symbols that the test subject would identify by psychic means. His 1934 book, Extrasensory Perception, was the framework for future ESP research. He presented great evidence and argued that he demonstrated the existence of psychic abilities. As you can guess, he faced a great deal of skepticism and criticism from the scientific community, but nonetheless, he did inject the subject matter into the academic community.

Coincidentally, right around the time of 1934, as you may guess, most things being researched were being dreamed of in a war-making fashion. This would be no different. All of the research into ESP and the psychoenergetic phenomena, which wasn't called that yet, was obviously under the watchful eye of militaries across the world. Then World War II happened.

There is a lot of research and speculation into what the Deutsch culture may have achieved, and that it links to secret space programs that broke off because of psychic contact with extraterrestrials. It's a big hat to wear, but there is some very credible evidence suggesting that this has happened - not just my account.

However, it cannot be argued that psychic phenomena and research were ignored by

governments. Many researchers have speculated
that after World War II, the United States took
the scientists from Germany who had been
working on the rocket program - essentially the
engineers and scientists - into creating missiles
and things that could access space. What's not
normally known is that many say that the
Soviets took the scientists who were working on
psychic research, things like channeling, remote
viewing, and the like. So it became a natural
progression for the United States to play catch
up. The Soviet Union had to play catch up with
space exploration, and the United States had to
play catch up with psychic research years later.

Operation Paperclip.

Chapter 3: Psycho Energetic Monuments

This next part is a huge curiosity of mine. Everything I've pulled together over time - trying to explain the phenomenon, learning the science of it, and talking to other people who have had great experiences, as well as running the remote viewing groups and a remote influencing group on *Talks With Tony* - has led me to this theory.

That being said, it's just a theory at this point. Importantly, there are things from this that you can do on your own if you're so inclined to get a little bit of proof for yourself. I am going into this because it really ties into the history of psychoenergetics. Also because of personal experiments that I found to have shocking results. We now know from previous chapters that psychic phenomena have been an integral part of history.

Everyone has a sense of awe when looking at ancient megalithic stone sites. What happened in Egypt thousands of years ago doesn't seem to fit the bill of the history of everywhere else. We also see similarities in stone structures globally. The official archaeological narrative of the Stone Age is hopelessly wrong in thinking that all these cultures were not connected; there's just too much evidence. Not only that, but the willpower, skill, and craftsmanship to construct all these stone monuments globally, thousands of years apart, suggest that there is a lot we don't know about them or their origin.

I don't think a lot of people realize some of the real advanced work in quartz that has taken place. I have to cite Marcel Vogel. Marcel Vogel was an employee of IBM and is credited with inventing the magnetic coating for the standard hard drive—a major breakthrough in storing digital memory.

After his discovery, he went on to research new ways to store memory or to store digital memory, which led him to quartz. There's a long story about the origin of his discoveries in quartz crystal. Marcel Vogel had been speaking about the properties of quartz, and people had approached him with methods of using quartz to heal that he didn't necessarily believe. However, when he began to experiment with quartz crystals, he made very startling discoveries. He found that quartz could change the properties of water. There is a very interesting article about it here.

https://marcelvogellegacy.com/about-marcel-vogel

This is a significant quote from that site: "**The water could be programmed with specific information depending upon the nature of the information programmed into the crystal. If, for example, the crystal was programmed with a sedative, the water would take on this characteristic or vibration. Drinking the water would induce sleep or deep relaxation.**"

Here is a picture of one of my Vogel Cut crystals - I have had stunning results experimenting with it.

I personally know Dan Willis, who worked directly with the late Marcel Vogel and introduced me to the techniques of using quartz crystal to amplify mental intentions by recording the shape of the piezoelectric energy that your thoughts make. By immersing them into a Vogel-cut crystal, it can project them like a laser diode. I have had friends absolutely repulsed at the talk of anything crystals. That is why it is important to realize that Marcel Vogel was a scientist that conducted measurable science on the issue. He performed laboratory-repeatable experiments that prove quartz crystal has properties of storing piezoelectric/mental energy. His Vogel-cut crystal, the shape he created by testing it with specific equipment, is very efficient at amplifying and projecting the piezoelectric shape and signature of intentions into water at a distance.

So what's the big deal, Tony? Why are you even mentioning this? We're talking about remote viewing, so why bring up "woo-woo" quartz? Well, "woo" ain't what it used to be, my friend!

When you look at the shape of the Vogel Crystal, it is cut at roughly 60° on one end and 52° on the other end—a male and female terminus on a crystal. Many have turned it into an art form of healing and other things. Everybody seems to want to have a hundred-sided Vogel Crystal as if that makes a difference, but Marcel Vogel concluded in the laboratory that the six-sided crystal was probably the most effective. After eight sides, it really begins to lose its effect, and after twelve sides, there was no advantage at all. When you look at the obelisks of the world, which I'd already kind of been a fan of because of the peculiarity of the one at the Vatican, I couldn't help but notice that they all have a 60° terminus at the top—the same as the Vogel Crystal.

I have long heard that there's a great mystery around the Karnak Temple in Egypt. There had been fierce debate over who built the temple. It's accredited to several Pharaohs, but it was occupied by priests, and the purpose of the temple, I believe, is still under debate. Correct me if I'm wrong.

However, the Romans and other invaders of Egypt showed great interest in the obelisks from that temple specifically, which were made of red granite, all quarried from the Aswan Granite Quarry where the unfinished obelisk lies, apparently because it broke in place before they freed it. Red granite contains up to 60% quartz content.

There's a famed story about the research that Marcel Vogel did. A wine producer had made a batch of wine with the local water from the tap. The wine was subpar at best and unsellable. Marcel Vogel used a large quartz crystal cut to his dimensions with a 60° terminus at one end and a 52° terminus at the other. He put a quartz spiral hose around the crystal and ran the tap water through it after he had charged the intentions, I believe of just "love," into the quartz crystal. The wine made with that water went on to be award-winning.

We also have hard evidence - scientific experiments done with silica in water and then treated with a Vogel Crystal versus the same water with silica untreated by the crystal. Put into a petri dish and, when dried, the silica is clumped and random in the untreated water. The treated water forms straight lines in the dried silica. There is a clear difference. This phenomenon is stated by Vogel as a piezoelectric mental projection through a quartz crystal.

What does that have to do with Egyptian obelisks? Well, considering the obelisks are the same shape as a Vogel Crystal - the 60° terminus with a tapered shape (however, they were 90° butted at the bottom.) And also, they are up to 60% quartz content - some of the highest quartz content in granite anywhere. They were all quarried from the Aswan Quarry, the ancient main source of red granite. So these are very specific, very special cut obelisks. Seeing the similarities between an obelisk and the Vogel Crystal, I began to look for signs of their construction or their sites that would allude to them being used for similar purposes. I visited Cleopatra's Needle personally in Central Park, New York, the first chance I got. While my own findings are not scientific, I can tell you that using it in person the way I would a Vogel Crystal went exactly as I expected.

I turned my attention towards Karnak, the place they all came from—or at least the place the Romans cared most about obelisks coming from. When I look at the site through the lens of someone who knows how to use a quartz crystal to imbue any given set of properties on a body of water, a completely new appreciation begins to take place.

It seems plausible that an obelisk with a high quartz content could achieve the same results as Marcel Vogel documented in changing the properties of water. He also made remarks on the field generated soon after "charging" the water.

Now, when we look at Karnak and the layout from the time of the first obelisk built there for Thutmose I (c. 1493-1479 B.C.E.) and then the second one built there by Queen Hatshepsut in 1457 B.C., they seem to be perpendicular to the Sacred Lake. Speculation, I know. However, the Thutmose I obelisk is about a half-mile from the Nile. Again, big deal, Tony. Noticing the entire complex is .72 miles long from the far east ruins to the Nile something stands out to me.

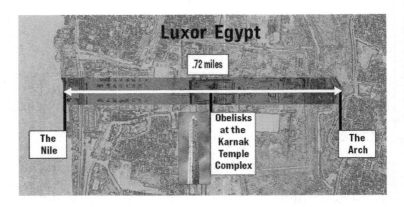

When you look at the layout of the Vatican Obelisk - from the Basilica to the Ponte Sant'Angelo running through where the obelisk sits it's also .72 miles.

The Boboli gardens in Florence from the top of the run towards the obelisk to the Pont Amerigo Vespucci also .72 miles.

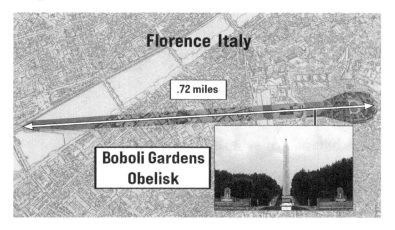

I could write all day on the legends of the holy waters that have come out of the Vatican, as well as Florence. And the quality of the wine produced in those regions.

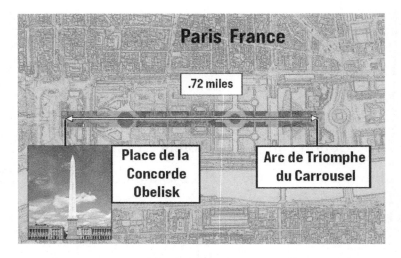

The Luxor Obelisk in Paris to the Louvre Pyramid, care to take a guess? .72 miles.

The distance of where it is implied the unfinished obelisk in Aswan and the temple of Khnum is another .72 miles.

 It seems that more modern monuments were trying to get in on the act. The distance of the military school in Paris running through the

Eiffel Tower to the Seine River, another .72 miles.

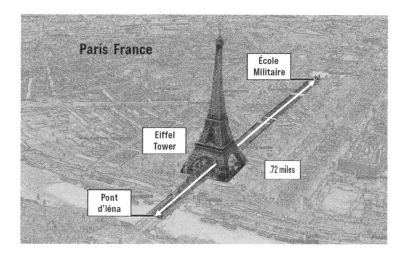

The entire stretch of the causeway of Astana, the capital of Kazakhstan is full of the same measurement from the Baiterek tower. Pools and the presidential palace all exactly .72 miles apart although seemingly a *newer* technology that doesn't have the obvious quartz component.

Not so fast!   The Monument Kazakh Eli.

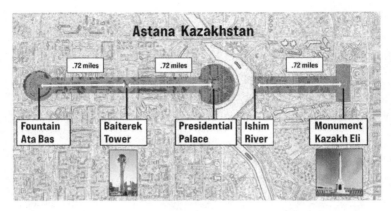

Even when the distances don't match, the same
layout with an archway or altar area then an
obelisk type monument and a pool surrounded
with quartz statues can be found nearby a river -
The Washington Monument, made from specific
materials that held up its construction for
decades. The distances of the Washington
Monument do however line up to .72 miles from
the end of the reflecting pool.

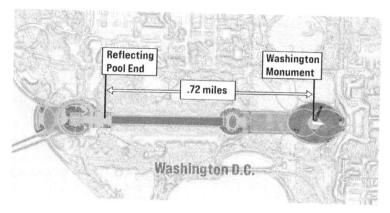

The St. Louis Arch is aimed directly at the Mississippi but is also .72 miles from the Civil Courts Building with its replica of the Mausoleum at Halicarnassus pyramid and array of columns on the top of it. Just for honorable mention, St. Louis is the same Latitude as the city of Athens Greece.

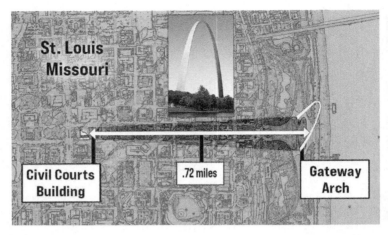

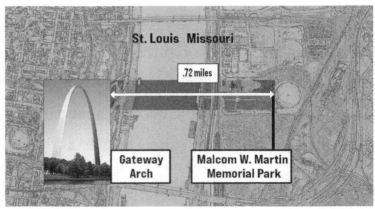

I have learned to follow the architects and you see the .72 mile distance with a tower incorporated often. Eero Saarinen, the architect that designed the St. Louis Arch also incorporated the distance and a curious design into Bell Labs in Holmdel, NJ.

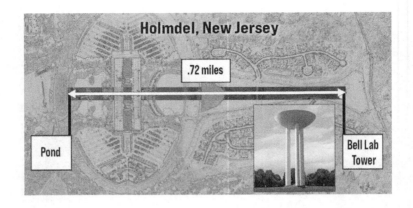

Holmdel, New Jersey

.72 miles

Pond

Bell Lab Tower

Also curious is that several of these sites have an arrangement of pillars in the path of the obelisk and the water target. They seem to be arranged a couple ways. One like an acoustic array. Another like a form of input or an amplification array.

Arrays In Common

Karnac

Luxor Egypt

Vatican

Rome Italy

Boboli Gardens

Florence Italy

National Mall

Washington D.C.

Why?

Well I will say my theory and move on. The same effect Marcel Vogel achieved of imbuing mental properties into water and changing the information band of the water on an molecular level.

I believe that was the purpose of the Karnak temple. That they had the knowledge and that the high quartz content red granite obelisks were in fact industrial strength Vogel Crystals of antiquity. Let me *repeat* this quote from the previously mentioned article on Vogels work and see if it makes more sense:

"The water could be programmed with specific information depending upon the nature of the information programmed into the crystal. If, for example, the crystal was programmed with a sedative, the water would take on this characteristic or vibration. Drinking the water would induce sleep or deep relaxation."

These are more results from that article:

1) water spinning in a coil generates a weak, but measurable field
2) crystals of quartz can be charged with "information" and tuned to the fields generated by spinning water
3) a critical charge is required for "information transfer" to occur (i.e. 1 - 4 passes around the crystal)

4) this number of passes can be modified by the programming of the crystals

5) more than one operator is possible

6) the program transfer is a resonance transfer with no loss in the original program after hundreds of experiments have been done with the system

7) water is made to be a permanent magnet. This field remains constant after the water stops spinning and can be removed by the application of a bulk demagnetizer.

The basic changes noted in water after being spun around an appropriately charged Vogel-cut® crystal were as follows:

1) decreased surface tension

2) the appearance of two new bands of light in the infra- red and ultraviolet spectrum indicating

a stretching of molecular bonding of the water. This is indicative of more energy and a new information in the water

3) the conductivity of the water increases

4) the pH of the water can be altered up to 3 points, an increase in acidity or alkalinity

5) the freezing point of the water could drop to as low as -30 degrees C

6) a significant number of the molecules would become aligned in micro-clusters or molecular chains; orderly, systematic and repeating patterns. The water has become a liquid crystal system capable of storing information

Think of a giant water treatment machine that is powered by a priest or group of priests.

All imbuing **ANY** intention they choose
downriver of the Nile in ancient times.

They could make the populace that lived off of
the water, for instance, motivated, solemn,
angry, or loving. Possibly called to war or to
peace. Improve health or longevity-the
possibilities are myriad.

Mass mind control.

Influence completely undetectable. The water
could be a transmission of thoughts. The
experiments on Vogel water suggest that the
imbued waters do not accept the characteristic of
the unimbued waters they come in contact with;
rather, the imbuement spreads throughout any
body of water with less of a charge. So, a cup of
charged water into your local lake does not take

on the charge of the lake; rather, the lake accepts the charge of the cup. Because it is a higher state of atomic spin, if you will. I am probably butchering the terms. Then think of the other places these monuments are in proximity to water and think of the populace being swayed unknowingly to one emotion or another.

Egyptian obelisks were all the rage for your metropolis, it seems: New York, London, Paris, Urbino, Florence, Rome, The Vatican, Istanbul, Cairo. Then the manmade versions: Washington DC, Astana, Paris. There are thousands of others. In fact, you can see strange-looking monuments in many cities that seem to be hubs of influence. Go have a look: Shanghai, Singapore, and on and on.

This begs the question to ask yourself, okay Tony, what if they are? What can you do about it? On the wild chance that these monuments are machines for some secret group of people that know how to use them.

Well, my amici's, if that is the case, then it seems like the clearing exercise described by Marcel Vogel may be of use. Just clearing the water before you drink it may be enough to subside the effect. Meditate and imagine yourself and the water as completely clear and blank. Compressed into one intention and snort out your nose. Sounds crazy, I know, but it works. You can use a Vogel crystal into the water and, using dowsing rods, observe a field growing slowly out from the water with new intentions in it.

But this is a rabbit hole that is much deeper...

Notice I didn't even touch the subject of pyramids with this!

So, yes, my friend...

Psycho Energetic Monuments

Exist.

Chapter 4: The 1970s SRI Research

By now, most people are familiar with remote viewing through the declassified documents and the method of CRV (Controlled Remote Viewing or Coordinate Remote Viewing) developed by the Stanford Research Institute. I don't need to list all the names, even though it is noteworthy that most of what we have today in the way of remote viewing techniques and groups stemmed from this government-funded research, initially through the Army. This research eventually morphed into something called psychoenergetics, which I'll cover more extensively later. It's important to note that from 1972 to 1974, the Stanford Research Institute (SRI) published an article in *Nature* titled "Information Under Conditions of Sensory Shielding." The article was problematic among

SRI colleagues, but Yuri Geller, the subject of the study, continues to use the publication as evidence of psychic powers. SRI had the Stargate Project, which began in 1978 and really seemed to shake the foundation of CRV or Coordinate Remote Viewing.

What a lot of people don't know is that personnel from the project went underground or into black projects, and that's where my testimony comes in. It seems they really took the gloves off for the following projects after Project Stargate. The initial programs would have been riddled with human rights rules and regulations for researchers to be bound by. For instance, they couldn't make a participant unwillingly take a drug or an herbal remedy or something that would be detrimental to their health in the attempt to make the psychoenergetic ability more effective.

All of my testimony, as stated in my first book, *Series Colony Cavalier*, and in this book, as well as in the many live talks and interviews I've done over the years, would lead to the contrary. The CIA and Army INSCOM found an "end-around" of clandestine black project regulations. They had access to what they believed were cloned humans - essentially children with amnesia, cloned by means of advanced technologies that our government had and, dare I say, traded with extraterrestrials to obtain.

The fact of the matter is, I remember it quite well. The research was very advanced. The players were there. I don't want to name names in this book because I have to be careful about what I say that could be construed as illegal activity. However, going back and remembering the buildings where the project took place for us kids possibly clones of kids, or members of a "20 and back" - when a friend of mine offered to help, someone very gifted in research entered a national database and began to look for the tax assessment of the buildings in the Inyokern Airport area. The buildings I remembered were portable structures stacked in a configuration that are now sheds, yet they seemed not to have a tax assessment. There is a database with a tax assessment of every standing structure in the United States, and those buildings didn't exist. Furthermore, they were classified as "California Special District" making them exempt from local law enforcement. In other words, if you were going to have a clandestine program with radically advanced techniques—trauma-based mind control, drugs, even classified things such as lasers that may leave permanent damage on the subject - it would be perfectly legal inside a building designated as a California Special District. In fact, local police, federal police, and even military police wouldn't have jurisdiction if they witnessed a child being tortured in one of these buildings. It was under congressional authority, I believe, that Special Districts were created.

This freedom gave them the latitude to experiment with remote viewing and psychoenergetics in ways completely unhindered by the strict guidelines of society.

Things that you can't get away with may yield great scientific advancements. The same way the

Nazis did in World War II on prisoners of war to advance submarine and airplane pilot technology by subjecting prisoners to decompression chambers to see how much the human body could withstand. It's horrible to think about, but in terms of national security and really trying to advance the subject matter, a lie at the top - which is very profound - lies behind the veil of extraterrestrial life and technologies that the government has access to, specifically through the CIA's secret space program and the military-industrial complex.

Behind that lie was the ability to access humans they believed were clones, with no human rights or future names. Who knows what lies the doctor in charge of the program I remember was told? Much of it seemed to wear on his humanity as he watched what we went through. He would often leave, as did the nurse, but he told himself and us very matter-of-factly that it was for science, that the research into ESP or psychoenergetics and remote viewing was very important and could benefit all of humanity.

So far, it hasn't happened. They haven't released a ton of technologies that would seem to foster our consciousness in a way that research from this program may have promoted. That's a nice way of saying he was delusional. All the data they kept was used for themselves in the name of warfare, personal gain, and clandestine operations. In fact, it seems they've moved a lot of policies in the other direction so that the rest of us - the main populace of the world - move away from our intuition and don't develop our abilities in remote viewing or psychoenergetics in any way, shape, or form.

You don't have to look very hard to see that the collective intelligence quotient of humanity is falling, not rising.

Contractors

All these things aside, the documentation I've been able to look up doesn't have a clear picture of Grill Flame at Inyokern Airport. But by my own testimony and by visiting there, I must conclude that it was the gap in Project Grill Flame funding during April 1982 to January 1983. When I look at it, the only solution for the protocols of the paperwork not mentioning this is a higher classification or it being subcontracted by another organization or a military contractor outside of Army INSCOM. This document shows exactly that. This picture I used in a live talk in 2023 in Orlando, Florida, for the Galactic Spiritual Informers Connection. This is a collage of a few documents that I was able to download from the Freedom of Information Act's website. These are CIA declassified documents which clearly state contractors such as the USA Army INSCOM, the CIA, the NSA, the ACSI, the ISA, and the FBI Special Services were customers.

(CHART CHANGE) THE NEXT PART OF MY BRIEFING WILL COVER
INTELLIGENCE COLLECTION PROJECTS, THEIR SPONSORS, AND OUR
SUCCESS RATIOS. IT IS IMPORTANT TO NOTE THAT ONE COLLECTION
PROJECT MAY REQUIRE ONE OR MANY OPERATIONAL MISSIONS TO SATISFY
ESSENTIAL ELEMENTS OF INFORMATION (EEI). THE IRAN PROJECT, FOR
EXAMPLE, REQUIRED OVER 200 OPERATIONAL MISSIONS.

IN 1979, WE CONDUCTED 7 COLLECTION PROJECTS FOR 4 SEPARATE
SPONSOR AGENCIES. IN 1980, WE CONDUCTED 41 PROJECTS FOR 6
SPONSOR AGENCIES. IN 1981, AS MANPOWER CONSTRAINTS BEGAN TO
LIMIT OUR CAPABILITY, WE CONDUCTED ONLY 20 PROJECTS FOR 5
SPONSORS. IN 1982, OUR PRODUCTION FELL AGAIN TO JUST 11
PROJECTS AS WE ONLY HAD ONE OPERATIONAL SOURCE ASSIGNED. IN
1983, WE RECEIVED 14 PROJECTS FROM SEVEN DIFFERENT "CUSTOMERS"
(USAINSCOM, CIA, NSA, ACSI, ISA, FBI/SS). TO DATE IN 1984 WE
HAVE RECEIVED 7 PROJECTS IN SUPPORT OF 5 CUSTOMERS.

ACSI, IA CONCURRENTLY INITIATED ACTION
TO OBTAIN SECRETARY OF THE ARMY APPROVAL TO CONDUCT GRILL FLAME
ACTIVITIES. SINCE THEN SECRETARY OR UNDER SECRETARY OF THE ARMY
APPROVAL FOR GRILL FLAME/ICLP ACTIVITIES HAS BEEN GRANTED ON 14
JANUARY 1981, 1 FEBRUARY 1982 AND 1 SEPTEMBER 1983. APPROVALS
ARE GENERALLY VALID FOR ONE YEAR.

Proof of External Contractors involved

What is the significance of this, you might
ask? Well, it establishes the fact that it was far
more than theoretical and that they had
operational relationships and business customers
along with other branches of the
military-industrial complex and parts of the

government that were paying money to have remote viewers either hired or trained for themselves. One has to ask: What does the FBI Special Services need remote viewers for?

This next document shows the gap in funding from April 1982 to January 1983, between Project Grill Flame and the creation of the new project (Center Lane) that gave access to all the technologies they discovered during their research to other branches of government, such as the Navy, the CIA, the Air Force, etc. Even private corporations such as Boeing were given access to remote viewing data.

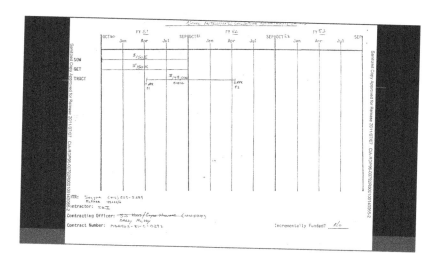

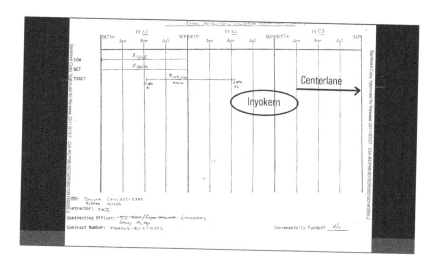

89

The date I was taken, as described in *Ceres Colony Cavalier*, was April 15, 1982, nine days after the end of the funding for the Grill Flame research. That means that a subcontractor would need to have security clearance enough to access secret space program-level technologies, or at least human cloning, and having the kids in my age group (10yrs old) trained and experimented on independently with SRI assets.

Again, when you think about the expansion of access to the research of remote viewing and then the reclassification of it into

Psycho Energetics in 1983 across the board, this does everything but suggest that it was a failure. In fact, it is direct evidence that other branches of the government could participate using the data collected and were eager to participate. Also, during this "downtime," a joint Senate Arms Committee inquiry about the procurement of participants happened from April 1982 through December 1982, led by Senator Claiborne Pell. This inquiry resulted in an agreement that anyone contributing to Project GRILLFLAME or the subsequent Project CENTERLANE had to do so on a volunteer basis. So during the experiment with children cloned or not, it was legal.

There were prior determinations about human test subjects in 1979, in which they determined the program to be "a transfer of technology" and therefore able to waive the requirements for volunteer-only test subjects. Allowing for unwilling and underage participants.

No seriously! Here is the document:

SGRD-HR   29 March 1979
SUBJECT: Minutes of Ad Hoc Subcommittee of The Surgeon
          General's Human Use Review Committee Meeting -
          26 March 1979

2. Mr. Targ and Dr. Puthoff presented the SRI protocol to
the Ad Hoc Subcommittee. Mr. Kramar presented the AMSAA
protocol. Subsequent to discussions, the following is the
unanimous consensus of the Subcommittee members:

     a. The Stanford Research Institute protocol was iden-
tified as technology transfer rather than research or testing. Similarly, the Army Materiel System Analysis Activity
protocol was judged to be phenomenological validation of
the technology to be transferred by SRI. Descriptions of
procedures and modes of evaluation are straightforward and
do not present any known hazard to the persons involved.

     b. For reasons stated above, Federal guidelines and
Army regulations on the use of human subjects do not apply.

3. While the Ad Hoc Subcommittee judged the current protocols as other than research or clinical investigations involving human subjects, sometime in the future it is possible
that follow-on work may be categorized as research, and may
involve human subjects. If any follow-on research should
involve human subjects, the Ad Hoc Subcommittee felt that
the Army sponsors and action agencies are presently unprepared
to address all anticipated problems. Specifically, the con-
cerns include:

     a. Provision for adequate scientific review of research
protocols.

     b. Provision for collaborating behavioral scientists
in execution of protocols.

     c. Provision for credible Human Use Review processes
or committees in action agencies for review of protocols.

4. The Ad Hoc Subcommittee recommended that the Army sponsors and action agencies make plans to provide for solutions
to the deficiencies listed in paragraph 3, above, in the
event that follow-on work is planned.

2

Bob Monroe himself and the Monroe Institute with their hemi-sync technology and they're out of body techniques were directly given access. Security clearance, and funding to assist in the research of remote viewing. Much more was discovered, or at least normalized, enough so to birth the term "Psycho Energetics."

To put it bluntly, the remote viewing program between April 1982 and January 1983 discovered new things beyond remote viewing and the CRV method. This led to the evolution into Psycho Energetics. They unlocked methods involving children, bringing them to near-death experiences with intense mental programming that pushed the boundaries of ESP into something completely new: Psycho Energetics.

What Became of Grill Flame?

c. (S/CL-3/NOFORN) To expand the operational capabilities and training beyond the confines of information collection into the field of psychoenergetic communications and psychokinesis. The ICLP will conduct specialized intelligence collection operations in response to INSCOM, departmental, and national intelligence needs.

2. (S/CL-3/NOFORN) PSYCHOENERGETICS (PE) include various processes by which individuals psychically interact with objects, locations, and organisms.

When we get into the more advanced techniques of Psycho Energetics and what they were looking at, you have to question what was possible beyond remote viewing. Beyond seeing target areas and extrapolating data from a distance, remote viewing was nothing more than a few people trained in a certain method of meditation and a procedure for building a file of information. What else could they be doing? At some point, they had to ask for more funding and provide some sort of write-up of what was possible to justify the expenditure and to see what PsychoEnergetics really could do.

Coordinate Remote Viewing (CRV) had stages one through four that progressed and whittled down more data from whatever stream it accessed, including other stages where they could make 3D models or very detailed drawings of the target. But Psychoenergetics is something completely separate. Here are some excerpts from a document of proposed further stages beyond the 1 to 4 of the established CRV protocol.

In the image on page 97, you can see stage 7 would be analytics. Stage 8 would be phonetics or sonics, which seem to be a logical progression of the method. Stage 9 was telepathic skills, also a logical progression. But in the following image on page 98, stage 10 was remote action, mind over matter, or psychokinesis, where they could move things. They had an understanding of how it worked and had every intention of altering and interacting with things at the target site, which could have been at any distance. Phase two would involve teleportation of items from the site to the place of the viewer and then back again. The science behind this was clearly theoretical at the time but based on Psycho Energetics methods. Established from what happened at the end of Project Grill Flame from one of these contractor projects where they had no restrictions on the subjects and what they could do to produce results.

Stage 11 would be altering the dimensionality at the site. This is the most difficult stage to understand, as it says they could alter the perception of time for the target, so someone at the site could perceive the passage of time as being much slower or much faster than it really would have been.

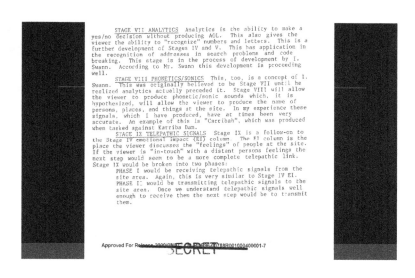

STAGE VII ANALYTICS Analytics is the ability to make a yes/no decision without producing AOL. This also gives the viewer the ability to "recognize" numbers and letters. This is a further development of Stages IV and V. This has application in the recognition of addresses in search problems and code breaking. This stage is in the process of development by I. Swann. According to Mr. Swann this development is proceeding well.

STAGE VIII PHONETICS/SONICS This, too, is a concept of I. Swann. This was originally believed to be Stage VII until he realized analytics actually preceded it. Stage VIII will allow the viewer to produce phonetic/sonic sounds which, it is hypothesized, will allow the viewer to produce the name of persons, places, and things at the site. In my experience these signals, which I have produced, have at times been very accurate. An example of this is "Carribah", which was produced when tasked against Karriba Dam.

STAGE IX TELEPATHIC SIGNALS Stage IX is a follow-on to the Stage IV emotional impact (EI) column. The EI column is the place the viewer discusses the "feelings" of people at the site. If the viewer is "in-touch" with a distant persons feelings the next step would seem to be a more complete telepathic link. Stage IX would be broken into two phases:

PHASE I would be receiving telepathic signals from the site area. Again, this is very similar to Stage IV EI.
PHASE II would be transmitting telepathic signals to the site area. Once we understand telepathic signals well enough to receive them the next step would be to transmit them.

STAGE X   REMOTE ACTION (RA)   Stage X would be
mind-over-matter, also known as psychokinesis (PK). We have very
little understanding of PK, but we do know it exists. If Stage
IX is telepathic signals which effect people, it is logical the
next stage would be RA signals which effect "things". Stage X
would be divided into three phases:
     PHASE I would be affecting or interacting with "things" at
     the site.
     PHASE II would be teleportation of things from the site.
     Teleportation is an element of PK. Once we can interact
     with things at the site the next step would be to "bring
     things back from the site".
     PHASE III would be teleportation of things to the site.
     Once we can remove things from the site we should be able
     to send them as well.
     STAGE XI ALTERING THE DIMENSIONALITY AT THE SITE   This is
the most difficult stage to understand. Time is considered
another dimension, but there may be many more. Mathematically it
is considered that there are infinite numbers of dimensions.
Stage XI would be broken into at least two phases:
     PHASE I would be altering time at the site. Time could be
     frozen, moved forward, or moved back. The implications of
     this are mind boggling. I believe this is the first stage
     where we could truly effect (alter) the future (as well as
     the past and the present).
     PHASE II Maybe by the time we reach Stage XI we will

TELEPORTATION!!!
And altering
perception of time
on target and target
site.

     PHASE II would be teleportation of things from the site.
     Teleportation is an element of PK. Once we can interact
     with things at the site the next step would be to "bring
     things back from the site".
     PHASE III would be teleportation of things to the site.
     Once we can remove things from the site we should be able
     to send them as well.
     STAGE XI ALTERING THE DIMENSIONALITY AT THE SITE   This is

As if this subject isn't mind blowing enough,

what I'm about to share may catch you off guard.

Altering site dimensionality is something we

never hear of, or do we?

98

Chapter 5: Protector

I first went public with my story in September 2016. By early 2017, I had been on many YouTube channels, a few TV stations out west, radio shows, and podcasts. I seemed to be doing 2 to 3 a week back then. One day, I got an email, and I don't remember now how he got my email, but he explained to me that it was from a friend of a friend or an acquaintance from one of the shows that I'd done. At the time, my email was private.

But it was a very strange email. It was encrypted on both ends, and I had to jump through hoops to even open it. It was somebody saying that he needed to talk to me badly about some of the technologies that I had witnessed. I set up a time for a phone call, and we did just that a few days later. I can't give his name or the name of the organization or the company he was associated with, but I can say that he was an ex-United States Special Forces operative. He was a privately run contractor with other special forces operatives who had retired from the United States service and become soldiers of fortune.

He said he was waiting on funding because there was a huge problem of human trafficking that was systemic and pervasive throughout the branches of government that we are unaware of. He asked me if I was available to be hired on as a consultant. I was extremely blown away by this offer. Firstly, it was validating-there was somebody inside a level of security in the government reaching out to me and validating my information. That was very emotional for me. Secondly, I had just moved from Hawaii to Michigan with my family, three dogs, three daughters, and my wife. We were hurting for money. I really needed the money at the time, it was a huge opportunity. It would have paid very well. So I considered it, and he and I set up another time for a phone call a week or two later.

In the meantime, I had been working with some researchers who had access to people on the inside in the military. I forwarded their information to see if this was legitimate. Through my researcher friend, it came back that this was a legitimate operation and that these were the real deal.

For the whole week, I thought about the possibilities and questions I should have asked. When we spoke again over the phone, I began to ask some things like how did this come about, what is the history here, and what kind of things are you talking about because he was very secretive about the mission. This is where this becomes relevant to this book.

He told me that they had already done a few live missions vaguely around the area of Central America. They had gone in and rescued a politician's daughter who had been kidnapped and sold into sex slavery. There were things in my interviews that he saw that he had experienced directly, and there were other missions that he had classified access to briefings about, which I am not going to go into. Frankly, there are some secrets that I must keep.

However, he described one mission in Central America to rescue this politician's daughter. She was in a brothel in the middle of the jungle, far from any infrastructure. It was a building set up as a brothel.

He said that each member of the team would go in separately at different intervals so they didn't appear to be affiliated with each other. The plan was for each to go in and take different positions in the bar. They were armed, and then he would come in and begin requesting services from a young girl. They would bring him a girl, and he would say, "Not Grandma, here, give me something younger." They would bring another younger girl, and he would say, "Come on, what's with all these grannies?" When finally the girl they knew was there would come out, they would engage, *violently* if necessary, and then get her out of there. This was the original plan.

However, when they got within 50 yards of the building, they began to experience what he described as walking waist-deep through a swamp or molasses. They couldn't walk steadily. The first man that went in could barely make it to the front door. He was paralyzed with fear and, or some kind of other influence causing him to move very slowly and laboriously towards the door. The second man went in and, being religious, said to himself, "In the name of Jesus, I'm going to go in there and rescue this girl." He moved freely for the next 10 feet before the effect set in again. He repeated the phrase, and he told everyone on the radio, and they all adopted that strategy and went into the building. Their plan went off as they had hoped, and they were successful in rescuing the girl. I'll leave a tidbit here—there's more to the story on how they got her back.

There were some very shocking details of the return for this girl, and his personal theory was that there were extraterrestrials involved. But what I'm getting at here is that this is a clear example of operational combat use of Psycho Energetics to alter the dimensionality at a target site. In the 80s, in the psychoenergetics research through Project Grill Flame, Project Center Lane, and beyond, it was clearly a goal to alter the dimensionality at a site - changing the way people perceive time and, in this case, even perceiving space differently than they would have organically. It became much harder for them to walk into the area. You can see how this could be extremely useful in many situations, not to mention a war zone.

It's important to consider that this effect was defeated by prayer. Someone's religious beliefs - calling out to Jesus - were effective. I'm not trying to endorse or sell you a religious belief because I believe that's something deeply personal to each individual. Everyone should find their own spirituality and stick to it. However, it was effective in this case of altered dimensionality at a site. We have to take into account that these are very skilled, highly trained individuals whose identities have been confirmed by a researcher.

We need to accept this testimony as something that's plausible at minimum. I have found documents suggesting that in the 80s, they were doing research into altering dimensionality at a site and even the flow of time.

Once again:

CIA-RDP96-00788R001000400001-7 :

STAGE X REMOTE ACTION (RA) Stage X would be mind-over-matter, also known as psychokinesis (PK). We have very little understanding of PK, but we do know it exists. If Stage IX is telepathic signals which effect people, it is logical the next stage would be RA signals which effect "things". Stage X would be divided into three phases:

PHASE I would be affecting or interacting with "things" at the site.

PHASE II would be teleportation of things from the site. Teleportation is an element of PK. Once we can interact with things at the site the next step would be to "bring things back from the site".

PHASE III would be teleportation of things to the site. Once we can remove things from the site we should be able to send them as well.

STAGE XI ALTERING THE DIMENSIONALITY AT THE SITE This is the most difficult stage to understand. Time is considered another dimension, but there may be many more. Mathematically it is considered that there are infinite numbers of dimensions. Stage XI would be broken into at least two phases:

PHASE I would be altering time at the site. Time could be frozen, moved forward, or moved back. The implications of this are mind boggling. I believe this is the first stage where we could truly effect (alter) the future (as well as the past and the present).

PHASE II Maybe by the time we reach Stage XI we will understand enough about alternate dimensions to use this phase. I believe there would probably be an additional phase for each additional dimension we discover.

I realize these concepts are difficult to grasp and impossible to believe, but, they are a natural flow of the signal and it is for this reason I included them. Only time will tell, whatever time is.

108

Chapter 6: The Lights Blinked

I am fully aware that my experiences are difficult for many people to believe. To be clear, they are hard for me to believe. That is why I am constantly looking into things I remember to see if they check out and, importantly, if they don't. I have expected things I remembered to be totally off and nothing like what I remembered. However, time and again, they not only check out but are freakishly, amazingly, exactly as I remember. The reason I am mentioning this is that if one memory is accurate, then they must all be taken into consideration.

In this case, for this book, what I remember is extremely relevant because the first stop in my 20-year abduction story was Inyokern Airport, California, as an experimental child subject for a classified subproject of GRILLFLAME from April 1982 until December 1982. This project, in particular, had some famous faces in the realm of remote viewing and consciousness expansion from the early 80s involved. I apologize that I am not going to divulge the names here.

I woke up in a portable building with no memory of who I was or where I had come from. I felt terrible - nauseous, tired, and incredibly confused. A nurse walked by and noticed I was awake. She called the doctor, who was the man in charge of the entire experiment. He came over to me after finishing talking to another child like me just around the corner from where my cot was. He was tall, with reddish-brown curly hair and coke-bottle thick glasses. He began to give me a medical examination and asked me a series of questions about remembering where I had come from. I had complete amnesia. He finished with, "That's because you are a clone."

Daily, myself and the other dozen or so children would be sat in chairs hanging from the ceiling in a separate portable building adjacent to the one we slept in. He would speak to us very candidly and openly about our circumstances and what was going on. We were the advanced operational experiment from Project GRILLFLAME. He said the funding was cut but that this project had private donors and access to a deeper level of technology to really see the maximum potential of the techniques they had developed.

He talked about the history of the program and how it was important to national security and to him personally because he wanted to be given permanent access to the high tech he had learned of, such as cloning and space-based assets. He was very excited. When he mentioned that we were a hidden remnant of Project GRILLFLAME, many of the children started crying out of fear that the name indicated what was going to happen to us. He immediately consoled us and said that project names had nothing to do with what was going to be carried out. "We weren't going to be grilled."

The program began with us watching movies on a reel-to-reel projector. They were designed to hypnotize, relax, and shock us, all in a quick cycle of a few minutes, coupled with flashing subliminal texts. Separate movies each day, sometimes a few hours of one and then another, always playing for their duration, and then the reel would rewind, and it would play again.

They showed cartoons, traumatic news footage, and strange acting skits, followed quickly by scenes of animals being butchered. It was not palatable.

After a few days, he began to administer drugs during our viewing sessions. We even had to drink our own urine to get a refined version of the drugs we were given, cleaned and purified by our own kidneys. It was absolutely revolting in the beginning, but later it wasn't so bad when it was ice-cold and chased with juice. I could give you pages of what went on, but you get the idea. We were being programmed, not in an enjoyable fashion.

To put it bluntly, the most important factor in a remote viewer being successful is merely that they believe they can. So it made sense for them to build a child's mind from the ground up, fully programmed to be a remote viewer.

They went into experiments in remote viewing quickly. The doctor gave us a long lecture about Buddhism and how our attachment to who we were was what suffering really was. It was bullshit. We were being tortured, and he knew it. At times, I could see that he struggled with what was going on. The program destroyed him internally as it grinded on. He learned many lessons in science but also learned lessons about his own state of mind. Even a 10-year-old with amnesia could see the turmoil behind his coke-bottle glasses and the erosion of his confidence as a man and a human being, watching what we all went through and became.

But the Buddhist lessons were followed by meditation lessons and card presentations on general aspects of "targets."

We had a simple set of instructions, and each day we were given a pen and paper and told to draw what we saw when we first looked at a set of numbers or letters on the blackboard. I remember asking for a pencil because I could draw much better if I could erase. He said he wanted to see every stroke we wrote during the process. They were simple sessions with long meditations. I would fall asleep and immediately be expected to write down information the second I woke up at my desk. Surprisingly, I did get usable data. I remember one of the targets was the portable building we used to watch the movies. He had been told it was going to be decommissioned by Army personnel, and they didn't know what would become of the building. I remember falling asleep and seeing myself floating above the portable building, which was completely on fire. Many of the other children saw the same thing but from different angles.

On a personal level, talking about the experience of this program is a kind of therapy. I could go on all day, but for the purpose of this book, I will try to speed through this.

He tried many different methods for us to remote view: recordings of the target coordinates playing over and over in our ears before the session, hypnosis recordings, standard blank-mind meditations before a session, binaural tones, drugs, individual monitors asking questions, and even long questionnaires while we were viewing.

Never seeming to be satisfied. He would come in the mornings, before we were on our dose of drugs, and talk to us very matter-of-factly, usually about how hard it was to deal with the budget of our program because it was in between the official program and what he hoped would be a full-blown, well-funded program he would participate in.

It turned out that the program did get a build-out and went on to become something very widespread in the branches of the military, based on what was discovered by children. Appalling as it is, I think everyone realizes that children have powerful, natural psychic abilities until they begin to socialize or grow to a certain age, and then it fades or is just tuned out. So in the realm of science on a military level, where life and death is the consideration, there is an argument to be made. However, history does not look kindly on militaries of the past that conducted human experiments. This is why I think that, for the purpose of research, they slipped this through the cracks.

Before you start to really hate America, take a peek at this document from the CIA database dated August 1982. It cites no definitive evidence but clearly mentions at the bottom that they suspected the Chinese of doing the same thing with children.

(SLIDE 11 ON)

THE RESULTS OF EVALUATED PROJECTS ARE DEPICTED ON THIS SLIDE.

IT SHOULD BE NOTED THAT WHILE ACSI IS LISTED AS THE OFFICIAL REQUESTOR ON EIGHT PROJECTS, TWO PROJECTS WERE CONDUCTED IN SUPPORT OF ARMY MACOMS, TWO WERE COMBINATION ACSI/INSCOM AND ANOTHER WAS THE MISSING NAVY AGE.

(SLIDE 11 OFF)

I WOULD NOW LIKE TO COVER OUR PROJECT BOOK. THE PROJECT BOOK ACCOMPANYING THIS BRIEFING PRESENTS EXAMPLES OF INTELLIGENCE COLLECTED THROUGH REMOTE VIEWING. PRIOR TO ITS REVIEW I WISH TO EMPHASIZE THE FOLLOWING POINTS:

REMOTE VIEWING IS NOT A MAGIC LAMP AND IS NOT A SUBSTITUTE FOR CURRENT INTELLIGENCE WORK. REMOTE VIEWING IS A HIGHLY CONTROLLED AND FORMALLY ESTABLISHED, UNIQUE INTELLIGENCE COLLECTION CAPABILITY WHICH HAS THE FOLLOWING CHARACTERISTICS:

(SLIDE 12 ON)   IT IS PASSIVE

TO THE EXTENT OF OUR KNOWLEDGE, COLLECTION BY REMOTE VIEWING IS TOTALLY PASSIVE. ONLY ONE CLAIM OF DETECTION OF REMOTE VIEWING IS KNOWN. CHINESE SCIENTISTS CLAIM TO HAVE DETECTED REMOTE VIEWING DURING THEIR EXPERIMENTS WITH CHILDREN. DATA ON THESE EXPERIMENTS

SG1B   IS

INSUFFICIENT TO VALIDATE THIS CLAIM. WORK TO REPLICATE THESE EXPERIMENTS IS CONTINUING AT SRI.

119

My participation would have been from April 15th, 1982, until roughly December of that year. By that time, I was field operational and shipped off for a stint in Seattle and then to my assignment in Puerto Tahuantinsuyo, Peru, in January 1983, which is named Boca Colorado today, in the region of Madre De Dios.

The Mother of God.

My duties during my stay in Peru were fairly straightforward. During each month, enough cocaine paste came in by the river on boats and when they had enough for a plane load, we would fly on a C-46 Commando cargo plane to Santa Marta Colombia. During the flights I would be wrapped in a faraday fabric and given in IV with a drug dose that brought me near to death for about 5 hours. I detailed the experience in my 2nd book Project Starmaker. The short explanation is that other intelligences spoke through me while I was unconscious and they would ask me questions about the mission and our safety. I was a field operational psychic at the age of 10.

But looking back to the training. They did not brief us kids much on what we were about to do. Frontloading is always a concern. But after all of the trauma programming and sleep deprivation, it was a relief for the most part that they got down to brass tacks. Standard CRV remote viewings. Then the binaural's began, and they were impressive!

Yes, Bob Monroe was involved and had security clearance specifically for the later program, CENTERLANE. However, the DIA

(Defense Intelligence Agency) had already had an eye on Monroe for some time. They had developed a file of his research unknown to him in 1973 and 74. He knew key members of the SRI team developing and supervising the research into remote viewing. So my memories of binaural recordings and the entire suite of OOB Monroe Institute methods are valid.

As reported in these documents from project GONDOLA WISH dated 25 August 1978 :

CIA-RDP96-00788R002000160001-3

SECRET

to be actually at the target location. The product of Remote
Viewing is usually only a graphic depiction of the target area,
whereas the product of an OOBE may include not only a graphic
picture of the target location, but also a record of subliminal
telepathic communication with individuals at the target location.)

4. (S) This office queried DIA as to the advisability of
contacting Robert Monroe. Individuals at DIA were knowledgeable
of Monroe, and stated that the CIA had shown interest in him in
the 1973 - 1974 time frame. DIA contacted the CIA, and learned
that the CIA had no interest in Monroe at the present time. The
CIA's assessment of Monroe during the 1973 - 1974 time frame was
very casual, and did not lead to any conclusions concerning
Monroe's abilities. CIA representatives stated that Monroe was
"OK" from a security standpoint, and they had no objections to
having this office approach Monroe. DIA also contacted government
scientific parapsychology experts at FTD, who stated that they
were most interested in Monroe's work, but had not, as yet, had
the time to evaluate it. FTD recommended that Monroe be contacted,
and requested that they be kept informed of any work with Monroe,
as his technique could have significant impact on their program.
(FTD has the mission to verify Soviet parapsychology research and
development by duplicating known efforts of the Soviets. To this
end, contracts have, in the past, been let to SRI because of their
success with Remote Viewing. SRI has not dealt with OOBE, even
though there appears to be Soviet research and development in this
area. This situation is a product of the 10 to 12 year scientific
lag in parapsychology research suffered by the US.) DIA then
queried SRI scientists about Monroe. SRI representatives stated
that they had not evaluated Monroe's teaching technique. SRI's
research is with Remote Viewing, not OOBE, and SRI has had some
success at teaching Remote Viewing. Scientists at SRI (Dr. Targ
and Dr. Puthoff) also stated that they knew Monroe personally,
and believed him to be a credible individual who has had parapsychological experiences which are not beyond present understanding.
Based on DIA's inquiries, they suggested this office contact Monroe,
if it was determined that such contact would be beneficial to our
investigation of parapsychology.

5. (S) This office then requested routine security files checks
be made on Monroe to insure his loyalty. These checks were
conducted, and no derogatory information was developed. Further
investigation of Monroe revealed that he has a scientific laboratory
known as the Monroe Institute of Applied Science in Afton, VA. The
training program offered by Monroe in conjunction with the Institute
is highly regarded by a number of individuals knowledgeable of
parapsychological phenomena. Dr. Thelma Moss of the University of

2

SECRET

123

26 August 1983

EXECUTIVE SUMMARY

SUBJECT: CENTER LANE Involvement with Monroe Institute of
Applied Sciences (MIAS) (S/CL-4/NOFORN)

1. (S/CL-4/NOFORN) HISTORY:

Activity with MIAS techniques by this office began in April
1978. On 11 September 1980, Robert A. Monroe was granted a
SECRET security clearance. After a complete evaluation of
MIAS, advanced training for source personnel began in March
1982.

2. (S/CL-4/NOFORN) ADVANCED TRAINING PLAN:

a. Phase I: In-house application of Discovery Series.

b. Phase II: Attendance at Gateway Program.

c. Phase III: One-on-one training with Monroe under
laboratory conditions.

d. Phase IV: Application of Hemisync tapes during
collection operations.

3. (S/CL-4/NOFORN) STATUS: Beginning Phase III.

a. Training is to enhance ability of selected CENTER LANE
source personnel. Training will be specifically tailored and
designed to meet the requirements of this office and extend
beyond the confines of the public program currently offered at
MIAS. Training is expected to last ten weeks and will include:

(1) Instruction in the use and application of
nonintrusive biomonitoring equipment employed by the consultant.

(2) Instruction in and the development of Hemisync
tapes, custom made for project sources.

(3) Instruction in monitoring techniques used during
the Hemisync Process.

(4) Instruction in the use of environmentally
controlled areas during the Hemisync process.

(5) Instruction in the application and interpretation
of information reported through the use of the Hemisync process.

b. Monroe has been paid $24,400.00 (ICF) for this training
which will begin in the fall of 1983.

BRIAN BUZBY
LTC, MI
CENTER LANE Project Manager

CLASSIFIED BY: CDR, INSCOM
DECL: OADR

124

This clearly states Monroe's participation in CENTERLANE, but the dates are from a time when the program did not exist. So, he had influence on the tech in GRILLFLAME at minimum.

There was a point where they intended for us to go out of body to locate hidden targets. The doctor loaded us up in his broken-down Saab station wagon reeking of motor oil. He drove us out to the northeast area of Inyokern Airport to a place where he had marked some mounds in the desert with little numbered flags. He took us out on separate trips, only a few kids at a time. He let us out to walk around the area and become acquainted, then explained that he had painted rocks in separate colors and would hide them near the mounds. We were to find each rock and report its color and mound number.

We used several methods over a few nights to find the stones. He would change their position each day. It was memorable to me because there were many people working on setting up the sound system. We each had our own set of military-looking headphones. They played the Monroe Institute recordings for an out-of-body experience, which are now well known.

The first few times, I just fell asleep, and nothing happened. Other kids reported experiences, and the doctor was very fascinated. It seemed like half of the kids could go out of the body within a couple of sessions. I just slept during the session. Although, during the first part of it, I would have a profound sense of isolation from the outside world, then just sleep. The final stage of the method he was experimenting with involved his own favorite subject, lasers.

In addition to laying on our cots with the large headphones, we would wear modified ski goggles. There was a lens inside with laser diodes going into it from the sides, each having a wire that ran together and out the side, down along the floor with the stereo wires. It was literally a mess of wires. Nothing was wireless; it was 1982, after all. This had my attention, and for whatever reason, I was not sleepy that day. I think they adjusted our schedule to let us sleep in for the latter part of this experiment.

I had become accustomed to new things presented to us in this program being painful, so my take on the laser goggles was the same. I asked him if it was going to burn our eyes or blind us. He said absolutely not! He was a physicist and had done all the math, assuring me it would not be unpleasant in any way. I asked if it would degrade our vision, and again, he reassured me it wasn't possible. I tried to believe him.

When the experiment started, it was late afternoon. The binaural recording began. It was Monroe's voice, but this time it was a different recording. After the first 15-20 minutes, the goggle lights began. He had instructed us to keep our eyes closed. You could see the lights flashing anyway—first yellow, blue, and red—seeming to flash in step with changes in the binaural tones. It went on for hours. The colors cycled, and sometimes the cycle changed. Always yellow, red, and blue as main colors, and then they would mix now and again. It felt as if the whole experience was on a playback that kept looping. It was completely disorienting. Once, there was a unique color combo of lights and then no light at all, but it felt as if something was happening. It felt like the effects of a cup of coffee in my head in an instant. The whole thing cycled again, and I got drowsy. The binaural tone got louder and switched to a new one. I kept getting drowsier despite the increase in stimuli.

Then, simultaneously, the tone got louder again and switched to a new frequency. The light coming from the goggles for the first time was purple. I found myself floating above myself, able to sense the room, the sounds, and what the people were saying, but I couldn't see. I sensed the other kids waking up to this state and then moving away. I remembered to look for the stones. I was instantly above the fence line of the airport, looking at the target hills a couple of hundred yards away. I had trouble perceiving myself. I heard some kids talking in the distance towards the target area. I instantly was near them and could see the hills and the small flags on them. I began to feel more like I was standing on a set of legs. I saw astral versions of the others moving around near me. They seemed to have been in cliques, and I wasn't. By now, I had a sense of sight and could see clearly. There was a haze over everything that was purple. The sky was black, and I could see the stars, but there was purple shining light on the ground brightly, as if it were daytime. I looked for the stones but felt like I was standing in muck. One of them said, "It's over there." I didn't see him or where he was pointing, but I instantly appeared over one of the mounds and could see the silver rock. I looked at the flag, and it was hill #6. With the confidence of finding a rock, I was suddenly able to move around. I saw two boys standing over one of the hills and approached them. I asked if there was a rock there, and they both turned to me, their faces morphing into hideous monsters with fangs, and they screamed at me "Go Away!" I pulled far away from the target area, scared of them. I was in complete shock, frozen, watching them from a distance. All of a sudden, something happened, and I was quickly drawn back into my body and woke up.

We were taken out of our gear and laid in bed until we were called to the desk for a debriefing. All these years, I harbored some anger towards those boys for doing that to me. Now, as an adult, I realize that the doctor must have put them up to it as an experiment on *countermeasures*. Because when I reported it to him he didn't bat an eye.

P.S. There were kids that had eye injuries that day. We didn't all have the same setup.

Another experiment involved oxygen deprivation by flooding inert gas into an oxygen tent we were all set up in individually. As we suffocated, monitors hooked up to us would ring a bell when we were near death and pump oxygen back into the tent. It would repeat like this dozens of times.

Fortunately, I was on the record describing this long before Hollywood depicted it in the movie Deadpool.

Eventually, the feeling of dying got stronger and stronger, and the only suffering I experienced was when I was waking back up to life. I remember being angry that I was being taken back into my body and not allowed to go. After a few cycles of intense anger, I spoke in an authoritative adult voice, "Hey, let him die or stop this!" I felt like I was in between alive and dead, in between an adult mind and a child's. The lights above me blinked violently as the nurse watched. She yelled to the doctor, "We have one." They had a brief talk over me and turned the oxygen on.

Induced near-death experience turned out to be the real psycho-energetic power that we were to be used for. Remote viewing was just the appetizer for an ability that came with being near death. A monitor could ask me any question, and somehow I would know the answer, all while I was unconscious.

I went on to be used for this ability for years after, for a businessman in the Seattle area and as I have mentioned, in drug running in Peru. They were adamant about me not having any sugar. That, and the method of giving me an intravenous drug, has led me to believe that it was a version of ketamine. There were reports of soldiers in Vietnam who were put under for surgery in the field. They used ketamine as an anesthetic because it didn't require heart monitoring. A phenomenon of the soldiers being unconscious and speaking out predictions about the coming days' battles that were accurate apparently caught the eye of someone with program access.

To sum up this chapter, the remote viewing research went a lot further than writing bits of information on a piece of paper. In fact, operational assets were working in the field in 1983 for a **subcontractor** of Army INSCOM that was running drugs through South America.

I am a witness.

Chapter 7: Public Remote Viewing Today

It seems that remote viewing has become a fad in the years after the declassification of the Projects of GRILLFLAME, CENTERLANE, GATEWAY, and STARGATE with the Freedom Of Information Act.

A quick search and dozens of online sources to learn Remote Viewing pop up. I have personally spoken with Dr. Courtney Brown of The Farsight Institute.

https://www.farsightprime.com/

Probably the most active source of public content in remote viewing. They like to do what I call "Aggressive target's" Not the typical target such as Niagra falls or the Staples Center. They do very aggressive subject matter to have their viewers peer into. Such as "The Death of Jeffrey Epstein" "The Crucifixion of Christ" "Jack the ripper" and many extraterrestrial topics. They are composed of what we call Heavyweight Viewers - Remote Viewers that have 100's if not 1000's of individual viewings under their belt and trained in a standard scientific way.

There are other groups open to the public such as the Future Forecasting Group

https://futureforecastinggroup.com

They have talented Remote Viewers that I believe use the AMSAA Applied Remote Viewing Protocol.

That method was developed separately by John W. Kramar. Spawned from project GRILLFLAME in April of 1978. The Method differs from the development of the CRV method and subsequent projects stemming from GRILLFLAME in that it was for tactical use. Such as targeting hidden assets in the combat theater. Yes, missiles and such. Also the goal was to have fast 30-60 minute sessions with an interviewer. Importantly it was to be done with:

"No drugs, hypnosis, special sensory (visual, auditory or olfactory) or proprioceptive stimuli, liminal or subliminal, electrical or

electromagnetic stimulus will be used in this
protocol."

from: CIA-RDP96-00788R001700210083-1

So we can assume those methods were all part of other protocols and methods being tested. There are absolutely jaw dropping YouTubes of Dick Algier from the Future Forecasting Group doing stunningly accurate viewing sessions.

The IRVA - International Remote Viewing Association is a popular organization with a deep amount of resources for all levels of remote viewing. Founded by the cast of characters involved with Project Grillflame and the latter projects.

https://www.irva.org

There are many, many more - Including my own group that I have started, and provide as a place to hone the skill and not in particular any one method. Half of the practice is learning the phenomenon and the other half is actively viewing to get out of the novice realm and into an expert level that requires over 100 views.

https://www.patreon.com/talkswithtony

So there is my shameless plug.

I want to cover one other thing about public remote viewing today. That is there seems to be a fad of people that have no idea how it works or how the protocol works and they are using means that are less than reliable.

Truthfully the phenomenon is like riding a bicycle. There are many ways to do it and many individuals can do it with zero protocol.

However to ensure untainted results, one of the essential components of being able to access the data and know that it is genuine is for the viewer to have ***absolutely no idea what the target is***.

We are seeing people self target. Either by using means of self hypnosis or some altered state. Tarot cards, drugs, all of it.

Then preaching about what they front loaded to themselves as if it is verbatim.

A viewing with front loaded data in any way must be* discounted *and regarded as recreational at best.

Chapter 8: TI3R

I met my editor and co-author of *Ceres Colony Cavalier* as well as *Project Starmaker* in 2020 when she asked me to be a guest on her podcast. Jackie Kenner and I went on to become very close friends and likely lifelong friends. During the first podcast we did, I was amazed at how well we could communicate about esoteric topics that most people are uncomfortable discussing. After we finished recording, I let her know. I said it was an enjoyable show and that I was surprised at how well it went. I meant it sincerely, because at the time, I was doing 3 to 5 interviews a week and had lost count of them.

This one was different. It felt like she really understood what I was saying. I mentioned that we should do it again and that I wished people like her lived nearby to have coffee with because the conversation was some of the best. She got a serious look on her face, thought for a minute, and said, "Like a show—Coffee With Tony." We both laughed and then went on with our lives. I don't know how much time passed, but she had me back on her podcast a few weeks later, and it was the same. When I said goodbye, I said, "Don't forget our show 'Coffee With Jackie'" or something like that. Corny, I know, but she was pretty, and I was trying to be funny. Fuck off. lol

Anyhow, it didn't take her long to set up an entire Patreon show - graphics, editing, all of it. She called it *Talks With Tony*. I was not aware of what was really going on and the difference it would eventually make.

We began filming shows that were interviews with friends I had made by doing other shows as a guest and from the speaking circuit on disclosure.

To me, it was a who's who of the Disclosure community. We had guests like Alex Collier, Jay Weidner, Laura Eisenhower, Dan Willis, Mark Domizio, Will Glover, James Rink, Rob Potter, Randy Kramer, Elena Danaan, and many others.

Over time, a pattern emerged. Jackie and I would talk about the subject matter afterward when we were not recording, and it would always lead back to the science or nature of the universe and how mental focus has an authority. The things she learned as a professional psychic medium and the things I had learned by remembering my time depicted in *Ceres Colony*

Cavalier, as far apart as those subjects were, would usually validate each other. We had the best talks when we were not recording.

After a while, we began looking at the things I remembered from Inyokern and the psychoenergetics I remembered. We explored how multiple people using similar methods in a synchronized session could affect great change—even remote influencing. We would always joke, "We need to start a group!"

Both of our lives changed over the course of *Talks With Tony*. We released the book *Ceres Colony Cavalier*. I struggled with my career as a floor refinisher and the newfound attention I had been getting from sharing my experience. She got married and shortly after was expecting a son. As well as moving into a house to be remodeled, she decided to cut the hours of the week that involved working on the show.

Just at that time, we finally summoned the courage to start a group for the manifestation synchronized meditation we had always wanted. We called it Tier 3. Or the hip way to spell it, TI3R. The first couple of meetings were a disaster. I had forgotten and missed the first one, and Jackie was sitting there without me and the group in a live Zoom. She stepped away.

I was determined that this group was something important to do and that it could be life-changing. A few years earlier, I had used techniques I learned to manifest a fast career change.

I had remembered the technique and was researching it on my own before I met Jackie.

The company I had been working from home for had been bought out, and one day the new owner, less than a year later, was found dead in his condo. I was suddenly out of a job, at a time when we were not financially stable. I didn't show weakness to my family, but inside I was in a panic. Our situation was dire.

I began to use binaural sounds and a mix of Etherium and MSM powder before bed, remembering the state of mind in Inyokern just before going out of body. I would clear my mind of all thoughts for as long as I could and then heavily hold intentions of finding work that would pay. I decided to really test it and set the goal at $100k a year.

The first few nights, I just went to sleep and had no real progress, but after that, I began to stay lucid in the first moments of sleep and in the morning before waking up. I kept dreaming of floating through a crowd asking for work. After a few nights of that, I began to see visions. They turned out to be prophetic visions of places I would be working in the near future. There was a permission granted; that's the only way I can describe it. After two weeks, I stopped with the meditations. I found work, and it wasn't what I was hoping for, but it turned out to be a placeholder for 90 days or so while a position that met my goals opened up, and I went there. I had seen all of the places vividly during those final nights using the technique.

So I knew this would work in the Tier 3 setting. The group in the first days was made up of people who had been watching me for some time. I was flying by the seat of my pants, assembling the plane as I flew it, as Jackie would say. The thing about it was that it was effective from day one.

We would choose a target to have a group synchronized meditation on, do it at the exact same time, and then talk about it the following week. We have been at it for years now. It works! We have had stunning results. People change social situations, financial situations, healing, ease of passing, relief from personal health problems, and on and on.

Some targets we have no way of knowing if we had an effect, but the ones we do come back often with jaw-dropping follow-ups.

Recently, for instance, a group member had a newborn granddaughter who had a huge adverse reaction to the early rounds of vaccination and broke out with severe, painful rashes over most of her body. The situation was steadily getting worse for the infant over four months. The member proposed the target for the group on a Tuesday evening, to which we all agreed to have a healing meditation aimed at this infant girl. This one was super motivating because of the innocence of the target. We had our meditation on Wednesday night and went on for the week, knowing that we would get an update at the following Tuesday night meeting.

The results were this: The day of the meditation, her rash had flared and gotten noticeably worse in the morning. I am sure steps were taken, but nothing that hadn't already been tried for the last four months. We had our meditation at 10 pm EST that night. The following morning, the child woke up with 80% of the rash gone.

Your first reaction might be that it was just lucky timing. I would have you consider this: We have been doing this with sometimes mild results and sometimes spectacular results, but always with results since January 11th, 2022—pretty much every Tuesday for two years.

Lucky timing? I doubt it.

Another side effect of the phenomenon that I have personally noticed is the revolving door of group members, which seems to point at an effect that happens. When the group consists of the same people for a matter of weeks, a bond seems to form. At first, I attributed it to birds of a feather coming together in this community of a very small specific niche.

However, when new people would join, I would notice the entire group sort of clam up and be less talkative in the sessions. It was as if the temperature of a warm room dropped when a new person joined. After a few meditations, however, the temperature would be right back to where it was. The bond, it seems, is formed during the meditative times rather than the actual group meetings. I know this because there have been members who did not join the live meetings in Zoom but still meditated on the target. When they finally joined the live group meeting, the "temperature" never changed.

Ultimately, group meditation is far more impactful than it would seem to be.

The Tier 3 method relies on meditation as its driving factor. To practice getting into a centered meditative state, we began as an exercise, and for the fun of it, to attempt remote viewing.

We started by putting items in a bucket in my garage and then everyone meditating and guessing the item. Most of the group didn't hit the target at first, but someone always did! They would get close to what the target was and especially what was nearby the target. On occasion, it was guessed completely accurately.

In the pile of declassified documents, I eventually discovered the CRV (Coordinate Remote Viewing) protocols. As soon as I introduced even mildly the components of remote viewing in bits of data, the accuracy shot up. For fun, I came up with a way to score each person's viewing, and that proved useful.

It really is a fun experience to have a group of people remote view a target, share what they got with each other, and then reveal the target. There is a game-like quality. Usually, the target is exactly what they saw, but they interpret it in a completely different way. However, the look in the viewers' eyes each time there is a reveal and they realize that they hit the target in some way is priceless and, frankly, very rewarding.

I started the Talks With Tony Remote Viewing Group. It has been running for some time now and gaining speed. I have been able to study many methods of viewing, targeting and the like. It's literally a superpower.

That group was up and running 2023. It has met with some great success and every week produces impressive results.

Chapter 9: Somnium Opus

I need to discuss a summary of one of the
more powerful psycho-energetic techniques or
aspects. Literally, 100% of mankind uses this,

probably unknowingly. That would be Dream Work. It turns out that we don't just sleep at night, and our dreams are not always just random fluctuations in our subconscious. There is a lot of science devoted to what goes on during sleep.

The militaries of the world would love to produce soldiers that can stay awake for days on end. Mainstream academia, the same ones that are now backtracking on most of the theories of consciousness, seem bent on selling us the belief that dreams are nonsense.

I am approaching my 3,000th consultation working with people dealing with long-term memory recall, and I can say without a doubt that our dreams are far from nonsense.

In particular, the ones at sunrise, usually in the theta or alpha stages of sleep, bear a great amount of profound insight. The people I work with begin to recover fragmented and traumatic memories that usually pan out when investigated. Almost all of them have these experiences in the moments before waking around sunrise. A strong, clear dream that feels like a memory leads them into a mindset to discover things they had long forgotten. It is easy to dismiss them as vivid dreams, but too many have been able to check out events in their early lives that match what these so-called dreams warned them about. Validation is hard to dismiss.

They are just now slowly reversing the theory that animals do not have consciousness, something that I have always found to be totally absurd. Proper observance of the universe seems to point to the notion that not only animals have consciousness but that everything does on some level.

From that perspective, it would seem that sleep and abstract communications are not only possible but necessary. We communicate with everything around us when we sleep, and most of it doesn't speak our language, so interpretation through abstract means is what we experience.

The famous Gateway Assessment document that has lit up social media has its own take on consciousness and the nature of the universe.

Many methods of meditation take advantage of the state of mind while just waking. It is said that many abilities, such as self-healing and remote viewing, can peak at this time. I have found that access to fragmented and long-term memories can be achieved as well, just as you are waking up.

Dan Winter of https://www.goldenmean.info/planckphire/ stipulates that sunrise and sunset are the ideal times in nature for longitudinal conjugate pump waves to be most plentiful and the obscuring effects of transverse EMF waves are minimal. This makes the conditions for mental pulses to implode and reach the exact size of the Planck distance, granting access outside of time and space to the infinite array. That is all a mouthful for stating that conditions to perform Psycho Energetics are ideal at sunrise and sunset. Apparently the magnetic layline environment is to be considered as well. Also an environment with lots of EMF and transverse waves can dilute the access to Psy abilities in general.Faraday fabric can do wonders.

So, dream work begins at sunset. Hopefully, meditation is a habit. At sunset, begin meditation and programming what it is exactly you would like to work on overnight in your sleep. Binaural beats before sleep and an intention held for more than 30 minutes can have incredible results if done every night for a two-week period. The fact is, we are all in some neutral form of communication with each other while we sleep, whether we prepare for it or not. There are many methods to learn and induce lucid dreaming. That is another realm of discipline altogether. All I will say is that access to the universe happens greatly as we sleep. Don't waste it!

The intriguing book *Stalking the Wild Pendulum* by Itzhak Bentov lays out properties of physics that would support the possibility of such communication.

What I am trying to say is that you already do a great deal of work while you sleep. Why not do it for something you consciously want?

Chapter 10: Countermeasures

The big question that was raised probably from the very beginning: How do we prevent this from spying on us? There have been heated exchanges about the subject of Remote Viewing Countermeasures.

There are great arguments to be made that it is not possible to hide data from a team of remote viewers. To quote Russell Targ, "the harder you try to hide something, the brighter it shines." My experience seems to agree with that.

However, there is more than one way to skin a cat.

The Talks With Tony Remote Viewing Group conducted a study into the subject after I had supported data from the testimony of Elena Danaan. We had done viewings of a target that she had said had countermeasures set up and could not be viewed. The description she gave of the target matched exactly what the viewers reported—but with a barrier obscuring the target in the shape of what she depicted.

We had to investigate the subject more. For weeks, I studied the theory of countermeasures, and we conducted efforts into it. We tried to obscure the viewer. We tried to obscure the viewer's session. At first, nothing panned out.

I knew that there had to be a method. Firstly, because of the Elena Danaan incident. Our viewers were on fire during that time, and 5 out of 9 had the exact same results. Secondly, because I had uncovered papers tasking SRI with discovering a method of countermeasures. So, there was a sum of money spent on the subject.

Possibly the entire Grillflame program was for this purpose only or at least, firstly.

It would seem by Targ's quote that he was leading public opinion that it wasn't possible. However, I had my memories of the two boys scaring me away from the gold-painted rock, and it all made sense that it was an attempt at a countermeasure against a high-level method of out-of-body target viewing.

The Talks With Tony Remote Viewing Group continued its experiment. We tried different meditations, different affirmations, and different types of targets, all attempting to obscure the viewer in the way that I remembered the boys blocking me in that one instance.

I had been using 3D virtual software in the Meta Quest to map out the experiment over time.

I knew it was a very important subject. The software is called Noda. Then they patched and added an AI generation component. I was able to search abstract notions very quickly in regards to remote viewing. Then it came to me after days of dwelling on the subject (and using the method of problem-solving while I sleep) that we were thinking of ways to obscure the viewer. Why not go after the targeting aspect?

We did just that, with conclusive results.

Using a scoring system for correctly viewed aspects of each target over months of data, an average threshold for an outstanding remote viewing score of 15 was established. On a scale of 0 to 35, the 15 score threshold was found to be consistent and better than a 1 in 250,000 probability for success. The group had never gone under an 11 and had scored into the 20s several times. Fifteen was the goal and was hit fairly often.

The first time we attacked the targeter, we assumed that the blocking team had the coordinates and a false target was projected by four individuals. There were 10 viewers and one traditional targeting person. The team's average score plummeted to a 7. The viewing was a complete failure, and the blocking experiment had worked.

The next version of the experiment assumed that the blocking team did not have the target coordinates, but just a general timeframe of when the viewing would be. The results were better than expected. The score was a 10, but the false target had overlaid into the real target data.

The target was the Devil's Tower in Wyoming, and the false target of a tiny island in the ocean had overlaid. The viewers described a tower in the sea. Again, a successful block.

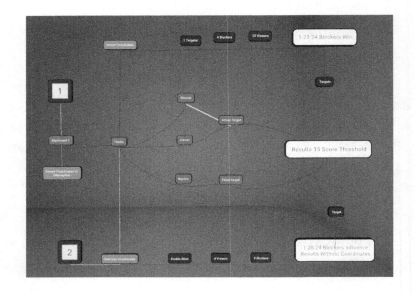

So in the case of remote viewing countermeasures, it is certainly possible to skew the data if not totally obliterate it. This is a reality and I am aware that there will be bruised egos as a result of this statement.

Early remote viewing guides recommend creating the target and viewing almost immediately after, probably for this exact reason.

The entire justification for the funding of projects that lead to modern day Remote Viewing protocols was almost exclusively for the purpose of countermeasures. Here is a document from later in the programs proposed for 1984 through 1989.

IV COUNTERMEASURES

    A.   Continue research into countermeasures

    B.   Design and test countermeasures

    C.   Implement countermeasures

V INTELLIGENCE

    Continue to monitor and report on foreign research

VI INITIATE INVESTIGATIONS into other psychoenergetic phenomena
    that may have military or intelligence application

Putting a search into Chat GPT for remote
viewing countermeasures (just for giggles)
returned chilling results:

" Shielding and Environmental Control:

- Physical Shielding: Using materials that supposedly block remote viewing, such as certain metals or electromagnetic shielding.
- Controlled Environments: Keeping sensitive information in environments that are regularly swept for electronic surveillance and other potential vulnerabilities.

Mental Techniques:

- Mind Shielding: Techniques where individuals attempt to mentally block or obscure information from being perceived remotely. This can involve visualization exercises where one imagines a protective barrier around sensitive information.

- Noise Generation: Creating mental "noise" or distractions to make remote viewing difficult. This might involve mentally focusing on irrelevant or misleading information.

Deception and Misdirection:

- False Targets: Deliberately placing false or misleading information in areas that might be targeted by remote viewers.
- Psychological Warfare: Using psychological techniques to confuse or mislead potential remote viewers.

Technological Interference:

- Electromagnetic Interference: Utilizing devices that emit electromagnetic signals to disrupt the perceived ability of remote viewers.

- Electronic Surveillance Countermeasures: Regularly sweeping for and neutralizing electronic eavesdropping devices.

Psychoanalytic Methods:

- Assessment and Profiling: Identifying potential remote viewers and understanding their methods and weaknesses through psychological profiling.
- Counter-Psychology: Developing psychological profiles to predict and counter the actions of remote viewers.

Organizational Measures:

- Compartmentalization: Ensuring that sensitive information is compartmentalized and only accessible to those who absolutely need to know.

- Operational Security (OPSEC): Training personnel in operational security to prevent inadvertent leaks that could be exploited by remote viewers.

Research and Development:

- Scientific Research: Investing in scientific research to better understand the phenomenon of remote viewing and develop more effective countermeasures.
- Collaboration with Experts: Working with experts in parapsychology and related fields to develop sophisticated defenses."

Not bad AI, not bad. This data is pulled from the internet, and I will let you make your own determination on how many of these techniques seem to be part of our daily lives. No matter how you want to slice it,

Remote Viewing Countermeasures…

Exist.

Basic Remote Viewing Guide

Talks With Tony Remote Viewing
Resource Guide

https://www.patreon.com/talkswithtony

Remote viewing has been
around for a very long time.
As such many different
techniques and uses are being
used today both professionally
and among enthusiasts.

This Group is the latter and our purpose is to explore available techniques and RV targets for our own indulgence. The reasoning being that the act of remote viewing is something that puts the user in a closer relationship with their own intuition which may be the most important lifeskill of them all.

For starters there is a great deal of established science

https://www.pdfdrive.com/stalking-the-wild-pendulum-on-the-mechanics-of-consciousness-e157830954.html

I very much recommend reading "Stalking the Wild Pendulum" to understand some of the science that goes on.

I personally boil it down to this illustration:

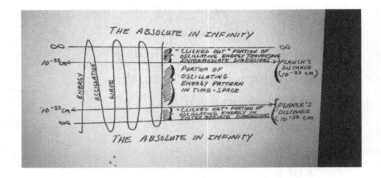

There is an app for your phone that can

help you exercise RV Techniques:

https://rvtournament.com/

I would Recommend reading some of the Russel

Targ works:

https://www.amazon.com/Limitless-Mind-Viewing-Transformation-Consciousness/dp/1577314131

https://www.amazon.com/Miracles-Mind-Exploring-Consciousness-Spiritual-ebook/dp/B003YFIW9Y?ref_=ast_author_dp

https://www.amazon.com/Reality-ESP-Physicists-Psychic-Abilities-ebook/dp/B00SKF0WLY?ref_=ast_author_dp

I think the work that He did in the early 80's with the

Stanford Research Institute and the CIA was really groundbreaking. I think you would be shocked to know how far it really went. (wrote that before writing this book lol)

I of course always recommend Binaurals - The Monroe Institute is the leader in the field by a very large margin.

https://www.monroeinstitute.o

rg/blogs/free-meditations/hem

i-sync-guided-meditation

https://www.youtube.com/wat

ch?v=ze2jcwu4ddA

The

heavyweight

champion of

public remote

viewing is the

Farsight

Institute.

https://farsight.o

rg/

Here is a great intro to remote

viewing on their website:

https://farsight.org/WhatIsRe

moteViewing.html

Detailed Remote Viewing Instructions Free from the Farsight Institute website:

https://farsight.org/SRV/index.html

https://farsight.org/SRV/farsightmeditation.html

This group will be basing many practices off of
this research.

This Resource Guide is by no means complete nor should it ever be. It is my intention to add to the body of work over time with our own experiences and knowledge gathered.

Your personal health is also important. There are cleanses that are recommended that can help any efforts into accessing a higher focus state.

Etherium Gold Focused brain can have results and
help you become lucid as you sleep

There are many attempts at monoatomic gold and other elements. This one is derived from a meteorite and has results:

https://healthcentralusa.com/products/harmonic-innerprizes-etherium-gold-focused-brain-60-vegetarian-capsules?currency=USD&variant=41655320641723&utm_source=google&utm_medium=cpc&utm_campaign=Google

%20Shopping&stkn=58c282dc
27f0&cmp_id=18295102456&a
dg_id=&kwd=&device=c&gad
_source=1&gclid=CjwKCAjwj
euyBhBuEiwAJ3vuofSaSBR0
mAGge3KWka9SJtoNZvD7S3
blkdCJ5BaDwLDqN9Wn_3UR
pBoCuVIQAvD_BwE

Diatomaceous Earth is a great Parasite cleanse that people should probably all do once a year Something like a teaspoon in a 6oz cup of water every morning for 30 days:

https://www.amazon.com/Harris-Diatomaceous-Earth-Food-Grade/dp/B07RV67ZNL/ref=sr_1_6?crid=EPDO1IJHTHU9&keywords=diatomaceous+earth+food+grade&qid=1676830479&sprefix=dietemaceous%2Caps%2C187&sr=8-6

MSM powder taken just a 2-5 scoop per day in water preferably in the morning can have results in making meditation easier to stay focused. Yes it is said to "decalcify the pineal gland"

but don't they all. I won't
claim that if I don't have proof:

https://www.amazon.com/Doct
ors-Best-Powder-OptiMSM-N
on-GMO/dp/B000BD4DIQ/ref
=sr_1_
5?crid=142QQJEVO3JE5&ke
ywords=dr+msm+powder&qid
=1676830625&sprefix=dr+ms
m+po
wder%2Caps%2C120&sr=8-5

Finally EMF Radiation.

Faraday cages and fabrics were
essential to remote viewing
experiments by the SRI and CIA
projects the entire time. Aside from
that in this day and age we are
bombarded with an ever growing
amount of dangerous radiation from
our technologies. It has been life

changing to me to start sleeping
under faraday fabric.

https://amradield.com/products/fabric01
8

 The subject matter of our group
is to remain confidential as well
as the results of our viewing -
They will not be posted into the
video library.

UNCLASSIFIED

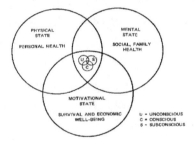

FIGURE 8-2   STATES THAT AFFECT REMOTE VIEWING RESULTS

UNCLASSIFIED

190

It is important to consider your personal situation when beginning any Psycho-energetic exercise. Accuracy can be directly affected by your physical, emotional and mental conditions. As depicted in this freedom of information act declassified document:

If you feel that any of these conditions may be a factor, at minimum it should be noted in your findings. Over time a routine may be able to be established to cope with life situations that may affect the viewing. This will be up to the individual to determine.

Here is a basic and effective method that is one of many.

1. Breathwork. Starting with taking 10 to 15 deep breaths and focusing your intention with every inhale. Hold the thought of a personal mantra such as: "I have access to all" and on exhale: "I will see clearly" This can be played with to find

191

something you personally prefer. Any intention you need during a breathing exercise can have huge effects on your personal health and a variety of other things.

2. Meditation. a few minutes of what I like to call a "Blank Mind Meditation" where you think of absolutely nothing. No words , no sounds , nothing. just an empty mind. Your mind will struggle to be heard at this point. When you have a peaceful feeling and your mind settles then you can easily access the target data.

Here are some tips to get there. You can concentrate on the Throat Chakra. The blue like energy center at your throat for some reason silences the mind.

You can also ask yourself when your mind is resisting being silent, "What will I think of next?" and your mind without guidance will tend to remain silent.

The Blank Mind Meditation is one of the most difficult to achieve. But possibly the best one for accessing the data of a remote view target.

When you achieve a state of mind that is quiet and less random thoughts are presenting themselves. You can move into the first action of the viewing.

3. **Recite the target** out loud as you write it down on a blank piece of paper. In the very instant you say the last digit or letter of the target - **Immediately create a scribble, or shape that comes to mind next to where you wrote the target down**.

This is an *Ideogram*. Many will tell you to predefine what each shape of ideogram means before the session and even practice them. Here are some examples or predefined Ideogram

Structure

Mountains

Action

Energy

Water

I have found in my personal
viewings as well as observed results
from
others that the Ideogram has   a way
of shifting
          towards the target, and as such I like to
keep it fluid and unrehearsed.

          Many times in a group
          setting people that were off
          for the day and didn't get a
          lot of detail about the target
          still had the same unique
          ideogram as others in the
          group.

          The point I am trying to make is that
          the Ideogram is the very first
          connection to the data.
          I am not sold on ideogram
          rehearsal and would
          recommend having a few
          sorted out ahead of time but
          be open to new shapes if the
          feeling is present to create
          them.

It is important to note that some of the best data you will get is in the initial few glimpses or probes of the Ideogram. That first feeling is almost always pointing in the right direction.

4.   After the Ideogram is established quickly *feel* for **impressions**. General descriptions of the target such as, big or small, hot or cold, loud or quiet, smelly or sterile, or any other types of feelings that may come. Is it an anxious emotion at the target or excited? Happy or tempered.

At this stage if these pieces of data are flowing write what you can as fast as you can. If you are getting very little or nothing and the data has dried up so to say. You will again meditate to a state of mind that is blank and not thinking of anything in particular. Now speak the target number out loud and immediately touch your pen or pencil directly to the ideogram you have written down. This is a probe and you just want to have your mind blank and open to the first flash of thoughts that come.

5.   Flash Sketch. After you have felt impressions by probing the Ideogram enough times. Make a sketch from things you have felt about the target. Don't concern yourself with it being a work of art. Simply sketch what comes to mind and put together the pieces you have already become familiar with about the target. Some remote viewing systems suggest closing your eyes and looking 20 degrees upward behind your eyelids and imagining seeing the target and using whatever image comes to mind as the sketch. I feel that this method takes practice dozens of times before it becomes reliable. The flash sketch can be done just based off of your feelings of the target from your heart or chest area. I think you will find that once you begin to sketch that more starts to pour out. Early remote viewing techniques would go a step further and try to make a 3 dimensional mock up with clay or other materials. this may or may not appeal to you but I would suggest giving that its own individual session after all of the data you can get from a viewing is dried up.

Repeat this process and whittle down the simple details. Doing this by yourself without someone to monitor and ask specific details can be a challenge to get to a high level of description. Some people make recordings to supplement a monitor. If this is something you want to try or if you have someone that can be a live monitor I would suggest that you make a few attempts on your own and build general data and then engage in a monitored probing.

In other words try viewing the target a few times and then do a monitored session.

Here is the bad news on multiple attempts on a

target - the more you do in a single day the less accurate the later viewings become. It is ideal to spread them out over a few days. the following is a template that is basic and easy to get some of the initial descriptions out of the way by circling ones that you may see. There are certainly more preset attributes you may wish to add.

6. A form like the one following can help make the process faster:

Remote Viewing Data Collection Form

Viewer Information

- Viewer Name: _____
- Date: _____

Session Details

- Start Time: _____
- Duration of Meditation: _____
- End Time: _____

Target Details

- Coordinates: _____
- Target Description: _____
- Target ID: _____

Ideogram A

What do you see? emotionally?

How do you feel

What do you Hear?

What is the size?

What do you feel? space like?

What is the

What do you smell? landscape?

What is the

What is the weather?

What words can

you read?

Ideogram B

Flash
Sketch

The last page is blank to have a space to add anything you feel is necessary. You would want to have many blank pages available and be open to making many different sketches or descriptions. This viewing form is helpful but only a suggestion. As you fill up the data sheet you can try to look at the target from different angles or distances and write that down. Also look at the passage of time and see the target in a year or a year prior. Depending on the situation of monitoring or self monitoring, when you get to the end of the viewing having the ability to be asked creative questions about the data can really improve accuracy.

7.   Targeting. This is the real engine of remote viewing. You have all the things I have mentioned this far at your fingertips behind a search prompt on the Internet. I have found that getting information on targeting to be a challenge. Many courses that you pay for will give a vague, quick description on how to target and then maintain making the targets for the prospective viewers. However I have found that targeting is most of the process. Also that there are a few different ways to target and finally that there are LAYERS to targeting that have huge ramifications on the data.

A: **The envelope.** You can easily write a question down on a piece of paper. Stuff it in an envelope and write a series of numbers or letters on the envelope. Give it to the monitor or viewer, and they can get a great amount of data about the target. A form of subconscious handshake between the Targeter and the Viewer takes place. In the effort to be a skilled shaker of hands It is integral to have the same amount of meditation prior to creating the target envelope. A blank mind meditation and then when the target is chosen and being written down to hold the intention behind the target and the curiosity about the target in your mind. Nearby the blank mind state. Hold the target curiosity in your mind all the way up until you seal the envelope. Also the more information about the target you can gather and include in the envelope the better. A picture, articles, the actual geographic coordinates, a question about the target, a statement of <u>why</u> it is the target, possibly <u>when</u> it is the target and importantly a statement of the intention for the viewer. "It is my intention that the viewer feels the joy of this roller coaster" for instance. Add anything else you can think of. Seal the envelope, write random numbers on the front and then try your best to forget the target until it is time to look over the viewers data. Share only the numbers with the monitor and viewer.

However when we are talking about accessing information from "outside of time-space" or more bluntly accessing everything all at once. We tend to get data that we have no idea of why it relates to the target.

B: **Layers.** This is a technique that seems like Pandora's box. It is possible to have 2 targets or more in the same envelope. With parameters defined. Before I explain, let me just say that this can be a great disservice to the viewer for them to collect data they have no idea about after the viewing and reveal. It is VERY important that the viewer be told what the target or targets were. You can severely impair their ability to remote view by not including them in the entire target reveal. That being said this technique is very very powerful in the things it can dive into. For instance you can create a target of the statue of liberty. Write your information about it and begin to complete the target packet. However on the backside question about the target, write something like: If my Mom is going to visit me this weekend let that be felt as a hot temperature and the smell of delicious food. If she is not visiting this weekend let that be felt as a cold temperature and a barren kitchen. I am trying to be vague here. What will happen is that a viewer that describes the statue accurately proves that they have access to the data stream (and by data stream I mean all of the knowledge in the universe) So if they describe a hot feeling with lots of food nearby. You can start cleaning up the guest room. Mom will be visiting. For obvious reasons you can see that this technique for one: Dilutes the original target data. For two: Can be used for many different purposes, some nefarious. Lastly: Can create an epic botch job if you are too aggressive, yield false data and possibly stunt the viewers growth.

KEEP ALL TARGET DESCRIPTIONS AND STATEMENTS AS SIMPLE AS YOU CAN.

Consider this, the Universe doesn't speak english. It communicates in raw data or emotion. Not in timely sentences but in bursts of imagery and feeling. Pulses at a time. A Simple Target will speak to this.

8 Scoring. It is necessary to establish a system to determine the success of the viewing session. In a group setting with several viewers it is immediately obvious that not only do some miss the target or ricochet as I like to call it. But some seem to have a clearer look at the data than others. It is almost always a result of the amount of meditation the individual does. In case I haven't said it enough: Meditation **Meditation Meditation!**

As such a method of keeping track is needed. Scoring can be dangerous because the first integral step to remote viewing is that the viewer absolutely believes that they can do so. Many low scores can discourage them and get in their head. There is an art to scoring. The viewing is artful as well. We are dealing with the right hemisphere of the brain that is accessing the data stream and the universe is abstract at that point. Making sense of it does require some personal judgment.

I tend to look for accurate attributes of the target that get described, and assign a point value. Someone describing water may have an accurate component of the target description but water is true of two thirds of the earth. Just water alone if accurate doesn't command the respect of an attribute like a gray couch or a marble statue. In the same glimpse of the viewers data these would receive a separate score. For instance 1 point for a nearby body of water, 3 points for a gray couch etc. Also I discard the false data or interpretive overlay and there is no penalty.

I have found that by doing this a set of averages work out over time and you can really establish a benchmark of success. My personal system of scoring works like this. However I am not going to share it. You must create your own and stick to it.

This is the basic outline of remote viewing. There are advanced stages that can be applied. Sounding out of phonics, using things like pendulums, The sensations of body parts. On and on, **but this is enough to get a great deal of data**. Also you can rinse and repeat and look at the target several times.

As far as technique aids, there are things like hypnosis, sensory deprivation, Faraday cages, and many other things that get experimented with.

To put it bluntly you will get out of it what you put into the session. Simply, the biggest bang for the proverbial buck in the direction of accuracy is - you guessed it!

Meditation **Meditation Meditation!**

Even the most adept viewers return to this. In fact they are people that can meditate naturally very easily. So practicing a daily meditation routine is the best thing to do.

Happy Viewing!!!

Tony Rodrigues

Bestselling author and secret program survivor, Tony Rodrigues now teaches remote viewing and remote influencing, sharing his unique insights and extraordinary experiences with a global audience. His teachings empower individuals to unlock hidden potentials and explore the depths of human consciousness.

ISBN: 9798327136038

Made in United States
Orlando, FL
07 June 2025

61919061R00125